COMBATING ADDICTION Through RECOVERY EDUCATION

THE C.A.R.E. PROGRAM

SUBSTANCE ABUSE AWARENESS
and
RELAPSE PREVENTION

COMBATING ADDICTION
Through
RECOVERY EDUCATION

THE C.A.R.E. PROGRAM

STEPHEN H.A. LLOYD

CAC/ACAD/ADSS

WE PUBLISH BOOKS

UNITED STATES OF AMERICA

Copyright © 2004 by Stephen H.A. Lloyd. All rights reserved. No part of this book may be reproduced in any form, except for brief review, without the express permission of the publisher. For further information, you may write or e-mail:

> We Publish Books
> P.O. Box 1814
> Palm Desert, Ca 92270
>
> www.WePublishBooks.com
> E-mail: WePublishBooks@earthlink.net

Cover design by Rhonda Clifton Lyons

Library of Congress Cataloging in Publication Data:
Library of Congress Control Number: 2004116001

Lloyd, H.A., Stephen
Combating Addiction Through Recovery Education: The C.A.R.E. Program

Printed in the United States

Combating Addiction Through Recovery Education: The C.A.R.E. Program/By Stephen H.A. Lloyd
   1. Self Help 2. Substance Abuse And Addictions   SEL026000

ISBN #1929841-08-6

First Printing, 2004

We Publish Books

DEDICATION

I would like to dedicate this book to my son Shane who has been a real inspiration.
Also to my partner Margaret for putting up with me.
I love you both.

And to all the addicts and alcoholics who came before me
and to those who are yet to come.
May you find the peace I have come to know.

ACKNOWLEDGEMENTS

It is not possible to acknowledge all the men and women who inspired me to take this direction with my life. Not only did their guidance and friendship save my life, it brought me to another level where I am able to share with others some of the gifts that were so freely given to me. I have been very fortunate in crossing paths with some marvelous people. I thank those in recovery, my current supervisor, teachers, professors, and co-workers. A special thank you to those who are still suffering from addiction. I feel your pain and I pray you find recovery if that's what you want. You are the main motivation for my writing this book.

There are a few special people whom I would like to mention:

- My friend Rhonda who helped in more ways than she will ever know.
- My supervisor, John, who is an inspiration.
- My partner, Margaret, for putting up with me.
- My son Shane, who for years was my reason for going on.
- All those in Alcoholics Anonymous who came before me.
- And my little dog Mickie for keeping a smile on my face.

To each and every one of you, thank you from the bottom of my heart. Without all of you playing the special role you did, this book would not have been possible.

PREFACE

Hi, I am glad you have decided to pick up this workbook and explore what is offered within these pages. If you think you may have a problem with drugs and/or alcohol, let me tell you from experience, you probably do. It is fairly simple. People who have no difficulty with alcohol and or drugs do not go around wondering if they have a problem. If you are unsure if you are an addict or an alcoholic, ask yourself the following questions. Has my drinking and or drug use caused problems in any of the following areas of my life?

1. Family
2. Friends
3. Work
4. Legal
5. Leisure Time
6. Financial

If you have experienced difficulties in one or more of the above areas, you may have a substance use/abuse problem. Please, do not despair. Read on. You are not alone and I am going to endeavor to help as much as I can throughout this book. If you find yourself getting frustrated, put the book down, walk away, and relax if you can. Then come back to it later.

Chemical dependency is not a new phenomenon, it has been around for years and years. Whether the sufferer struggles with alcoholism or drug addiction the results are the same, tragic. The C.A.R.E. program was originally developed to be utilized in a group setting. The program was designed to be presented by a trained facilitator to ten or twelve group participants. Although this method has proved to be successful, it has become evident to me that in order to reach as many people as possible, this program had to become available in different formats. Not everyone is comfortable in a group setting, or for one reason or another, they cannot get to where a group is offered. Thus, the development of this workbook.

Some of the work you are about to do may seem difficult, but please stay with it. The journey you will be embarking on will be a foundation upon which, if so desired, a new life can be formed.

If you are still reading I am going to assume that you are serious about making some positive changes in your life. So let's get started. I am going to begin by telling you a little about myself. Oh ya, if you haven't already guessed, not only am I a certified addictions counselor, I am also a recovered alcoholic and drug addict. If you are afflicted with some form of chemical dependency I am sure you will be able to relate to at least a portion of my story.

TABLE OF CONTENTS

Dedication   *vii*
Acknowledgements   *ix*
Preface   *xi*

	Author's Biography – One Man's Story	1
	Welcome To The C.A.R.E. Program	21
Chapter 1	Definitions/What Causes Addiction	23
Chapter 2	Classifications of Drugs	29
Chapter 3	The Early Going/Getting Medical Help	33
Chapter 4	Harmful Effects Of Alcohol/Heroin/Cocaine/ And Marijuana	37
Chapter 5	Decisional Balance/Personal Exercise	45
Chapter 6	What Is Denial/How To Overcome It	49
Chapter 7	Why Is Sobriety Important To Me	55
Chapter 8	Post Acute Withdrawal	59
Chapter 9	Triggers And How To Combat Them	63
Chapter 10	Is Change Possible	71
Chapter 11	Negative Feelings, Values, And Substance Use	75
Chapter 12	Seeking Support	83
Chapter 13	Goal Setting	89
Chapter 14	Anger Management	97
Chapter 15	Conflict Resolution	107
Chapter 16	Communication	111
Chapter 17	Dealing With Resentment	117
Chapter 18	Relapse Prevention Plan	121
Chapter 19	Journaling	131

ONE MAN'S STORY

A JOURNEY OF RECOVERY FROM ALCOHOLISM, DRUG ADDICTION AND CHILDHOOD SEXUAL ABUSE

Steve Lloyd
2004

ONE MAN'S STORY

A JOURNEY OF RECOVERY FROM ALCOHOLISM, DRUG ADDICTION AND CHILDHOOD SEXUAL ABUSE

My name is Steve and I am a recovered alcoholic and drug addict. I have lived through much adversity in the past. I have struggled with alcoholism, and drug addiction. I have lived through cancer and most recently the memories have surfaced of all the childhood sexual abuse I was forced to endure. There have been times in my life when it all became too much and I did not think I could go on or even have the desire to do so. My recovery has been a long and very difficult process, not only for myself, but for those who loved and cared about me, also for those who tried to love me and I would not let get close enough. Today my life is totally different, I still struggle from time to time, but it is during these struggles that one grows and becomes a happier, healthy, and functional person.

The reason for writing this autobiography is two fold. Firstly, it is therapeutic for me. Sometimes I tend to forget where I came from and how far I have come over the years. Secondly, by sharing my experience, strength, and hope, perhaps someone else may receive a glimmer of hope that will help take them from the darkness into the light.

As I write this I am in awe of my surroundings. I am sitting on my couch, a hockey game on the television, and in the corner a beautifully decorated Christmas tree with a spattering of gifts under it. Our little dog just went to sleep beside me, and the cat has walked into the living room to see what, if anything is going on. Sounds nice eh? Well it is, but believe me it hasn't always been like this. Things were once much different. Let me try and explain.

I suppose the best way to go about this is to tell you what it was like, what happened, and what it's like now. The only way I know of to do this is start at the beginning. I have very few memories of my life before the age of twelve. The only memories I do have are memories of my being afraid and very insecure. I was afraid of everything. From being left alone to getting lost in a department store. It is only recently that I have realized that all of the memories of my early years are fear based. I am one of those who had to get outside help to come to grips with a lot of this. How sad when the only memories one has of their childhood are full of fear. I now know why I was so full of fear as a child and I will get to that later.

I grew up in a family where drinking was a way of life. As a young child I learned that drinking was how you socialized. Growing up I learned that a man worked hard, drank hard, and basically did whatever he wanted to. I learned all this from my family of origin, especially my father. Don't get me wrong, my father was a very loving man, he loved his children, he just didn't always know how to express it. His idea of quality time was my sitting in his car in the legion parking lot reading a ten-cent comic book while he drank with his buddies. He too was an alcoholic and he lived his life the only way he knew how. That and I don't believe he would of changed it even if he could have. I followed in my father's footsteps only about 10 times worse.

The first time I remember getting drunk I was about 9 years old. It happened at a family Wedding reception at a restaurant near where I spent my formative years. The adults were drinking and someone kept giving me champagne. I got loaded and one of the adults took me outside to walk it off. I remember nothing else until the next morning. I was a blackout drinker right from the beginning.

I also remember my parents having house parties. Every-time someone would get up to dance or went to the washroom I would sneak over and help myself to whatever they were drinking. Either everyone ignored what I was doing or they just didn't care. Now I was about 12 years of age and I drank every opportunity I could. I would steal it from my father's bar stock or my buddies would get their hands on some booze somehow. I felt I had found the key to life. After living my whole life in fear I had found the answer. A few drinks and I was confident, assertive, better looking, ten feet tall and bullet proof. The fear simply melted away. I was in love and my love came in a bottle.

I'm not clear on the exact age but I was around thirteen when I was arrested for being a minor in possession of alcohol and being drunk in a public place. I have no idea how the cops even saw me let alone catch me. Some buddies and I were raising hell in a local Park. Ten acres of bush, it was dark, and I ran into a cop. That was just the beginning of my life and luck with alcohol.

At age fourteen my Father bought a boat (I believe thinking it would bring him and I closer together) and we had it moored at a local marina near where we lived. I landed a job working on the fuel dock. That was absolutely perfect for a young alcoholic. I got to know everyone who had a boat there, and I knew who drank and kept alcohol on their boats. At night my buddies and I would go back to the marina, sneak on their boats and steal their booze. Between that source and our friendly bootlegger we had all the alcohol we could drink.

When I was in my early teens my entire social life was centered around alcohol. If you didn't drink I didn't hang out with you. I admired the rebels and did my best to fit in. All we did every weekend was drink. I would drink till the booze was gone or I'd pass out. I also injured my leg quite seriously and wound up with gangrene at age fourteen. I came within twenty-four hours of losing my leg from the knee down. This was also the age when I met my first serious girlfriend. That started a chain of one girlfriend after the next. Relationships soon began to be a source of additional pain for me. They never lasted long because even as a young teenager alcohol had me in it's control. Drinking was far more important to me than any relationship.

At age sixteen I got my drivers license. Being able to drive was a huge confidence booster for me; I loved being able to drive. Thirty short days after I had my license I received my first charge for impaired driving. I was getting into a Hotel close to where I lived. The owner did not care how old you were as long as you had money. I closed the place down one night and was driving up a hill beside the hotel. All of a sudden the red and blue lights came on behind me. I stopped and like the good guy I thought I was, I got out of my truck and went to meet the officer half way. The only thing was I forgot to put the truck in gear. It rolled backwards down the hill and crashed into the front end of the police car. I mean destroyed it. My truck had a big checker plate bumper on the back.

I must have blacked out because the next thing I knew I woke up in jail. I was the first customer at the new city jail. No prize, no parade, no ribbon, although I did get my picture taken. I do remember being terribly sick the next morning. Somehow I got to work, I don't remember how. I was pumping gas at a service station. I remember my Father came in to buy fuel. I told him what happened. All he said was, "if you are going to drink and drive, drink vodka, the cops can't smell it". He was an alcoholic himself who was in denial about his condition. If he didn't acknowledge my alcoholism he didn't have to look at his. I received a fine and lost my license for six months. Right after I got my license back I continued to drink and drive.

I sold that truck and bought a 1962 Ford Galaxy. You see I had already begun to change vehicles frequently, thinking I could throw the police off if they didn't know what I was driving. One night some buddies and I were sitting in my car outside a school dance, being cool, having a few beers, and munching on a few magic mushrooms. By now I had made a name for myself with the local law enforcement. Well, again the police pull up behind me, I panicked, mushrooms oh no, what to do? So I ate all that we had. The police found the beer, found we were under age, set my buddies loose, and took me to jail. Well, once again they called my Father and said, "We have your son here, again. Would you come get him?" He did and to my surprise he allowed me to drive my car home. I remember it was pouring rain. I was driving along when the mushrooms began to take affect. I was hallucinating. The raindrops all of a sudden became the size of basketballs. The hallucinations freaked me out. I decided right there and then that I was sticking to booze. After all, the bottle was my first love and it didn't it turn raindrops into basketballs. That other stuff was just too weird for me. From then on the only mushrooms I ever had were on my steak.

The next few years, fourteen to be exact are a bit of a blur. In 1976 I developed a very sore hip. The pain was so severe that I could barely stand it. It was excruciating. My family doctor could not figure out the cause so he sent me to a specialist. The specialist decided to do some exploratory surgery. So they opened it up and closed it again right away. I had a type of cancer that left me with a tumor in the bone (Ewing's sarcoma). I began chemotherapy right away and then went onto a massive dose of radiation treatments. I was in and out of the hospital for most of the next year. Even though there were lots of people who wanted to help, I always drove myself into the cancer clinic, got my treatment, and drove home.

Driving home from the hospital I would be vomiting from the chemotherapy treatments. Still, I wasn't going to have anyone drive me. That was like giving up. To this I day feel nauseous whenever I drive over the bridge that leads to the cancer clinic. I think the most traumatic part was when all my hair fell out. For a young guy who so desperately wanted to be cool and fit in the hair loss was devastating. I went and bought this wig, kind of funny as I look back on it now. It looked like one of those string mops that had washed one too many floors.

It is obvious to me that even back then I had a strong belief in a power greater than myself. I was told later that the doctors had only given me a 15% chance of survival. I'm sure members of my family thought I was going to die, but I never even considered it. I kept working, pumping gas again. I also kept drinking. The chemotherapy was really interfering with my drinking as I would try to drink, throw up the first one or two but then they would start to stay down. The radiation treatments I had burned my bladder so bad that I was passing blood clots that felt like razor blades on their way out. I could hardly get up and walk around. I remember one evening sitting in a recliner drinking a case of beer. I would finish a beer and then urinate into the bottle so I did not have to get up, move around, and aggravate my condition. Nothing took a back seat to my drinking, certainly not pain.

I used to wonder why I was spared from death. Why me. The way I see it, the God of my understanding wasn't finished with me yet. I still had more to do. I now know that my purpose and reason for being kept alive is to pass the message of recovery to those who still suffer. I am very grateful just to be sitting here writing this. Sometimes when I get caught up in the little things I forget to be grateful and I complain and whine, but I really don't have anything to complain about. I have now been in remission for 27 years from cancer. My alcoholism has been in remission for 13 years as of February 28/04.

After they pronounced me in remission from cancer I moved north and worked in a mine for about 4 months. This was great as the mine bus picked us up at a bar and dropped us off there after shift. When the mine went on strike I quit and went further west where I worked in a sawmill. My drinking was just steadily increasing. Work to me was just a means of keeping a roof over my head and booze in my belly. After about 10 months I moved back to my old hometown. I was already running away, trying the geographical cure without realizing what I was doing. Hoping that when I got to the next town things would be better, at least different.

Now it is approximately 1978/79. A very significant part of my story is that I also got my self-esteem, self worth, and feelings of security from relationships. I didn't feel whole or secure unless I was in a relationship. I also confused sex and love, which I have learned are two separate things yet are a wonderful part of each other. This combined with the message I received about what it means to be a man resulted in my getting married when I was nineteen, far before I was ready to take on the roll of husband. I had known my wife briefly when I was fourteen, then we drifted apart. We met up again and decided to tie the knot. That marriage was doomed right from the start, my drinking saw to that.

While I was in that marriage I got my second impaired driving charge. I was far more interested in being out drinking with my friends than I was interested in spending any time with my wife. We separated after about six months of marriage.

I had been in a few serious car accidents by now. Somebody or something was looking after me right from the beginning. I was twenty years of age and should have been killed or permanently injured many times over. That or been locked up for drinking and driving. That's what I'd do, I drank all the time so I had to drink and drive. Besides I was often too drunk to walk.

I began working for a Utility Company. At the Utility Company we were all drunks. My superintendent was the worst. One day, for some unknown reason he fired me. I got angry, left and went to the bar. I had a couple of doubles and then went back to the shop in order to turn in my pager and keys. When I got back to work my supervisor wanted to know where I had been. I said, "I left because you fired me. Here's my keys and pager and you can shove them wherever they'll fit". He said, "what are you talking about, I never fired you". He was in a blackout and did not remember firing me. He constantly functioned in a blackout while at work. I shoved my keys back in my pocket and went back to my job. Nothing was ever said about it again.

I had another foreman that I would drink with almost every weekend. We'd sit around his kitchen table and drink until we passed out. Now that's good living. Anyway, every Friday night about midnight we'd get in a huge argument. I'd slam my pager down and quit. Next Monday when we were sober we would go back to work like nothing happened.

There is one incident that really comes to mind. It happened on a Saturday afternoon. There was one particular bar my buddies and I drank in all the time. I'm sure we helped pay for that place many times over. We would be there by 10:45 a.m. waiting for the place to open at 11:00. This one particular day we got into drinking double vodka tonics. Don't ask me why, I didn't care for vodka that much. Sometime in the afternoon we got cut off and thrown out.

After we got thrown out of the bar we climbed in my friend's jeep and drove away. No top or doors on the jeep and no seat belts. He took this corner and later he said he had just hit third gear when out the side I went. I must have passed out and fallen out the side. The owner of the bar was going the other way and saw the whole thing. He stopped and put me in the back of his pick up and took me to the hospital. I had a broken collarbone, broken nose, no hide on the left side of my face, and my body was all bruised. Again, I should have died but was spared. I have lost count of the injuries I sustained while drinking. There were several other broken bones. My nose was broken a few times. The bones and scars healed. What I was left with was a broken spirit that haunted me.

Now I am about 22 and drinking harder than ever. I continued to drink and drive.
One night I was staying at my sister's place. I forget why. I went out to this local bar for a few. Well a few turned into a few dozen. I met this very nice young lady that I used to go to school with. As usual I don't remember too much. I remember waking up on my sister's couch the next morning, sick as usual only this time was different. My sister and her family were all in the living room laughing at me. I open one eye and look around the room, surveying my situation. I looked down and I began to get a picture of what they were laughing at. There was my, (blush) underwear hanging out of my shirt pocket and I had on pink socks. Now these socks obviously were not mine so I still think they snuck in the

middle of the night and changed my socks. The underwear I just can't explain. That's what happens I guess when you get dressed in the dark. I was continually doing things to embarrass myself, for a while you laugh it off. But it hurts inside.

Alcohol is so cunning baffling and powerful. Even with all that had happened to me so far I still loved it. I was always trying to think ahead to where my next drink was coming from. I would plan my days and evenings around alcohol, making sure that I would be able to drink wherever I went. I was still full of fear and for now the alcohol continued to take the fear away. It still gave me what I needed. I never looked at the negatives. I only worried about where the next drink was coming from.

I met my second wife one Saturday afternoon. I was living with a buddy when my soon to be wife was walking down the road with her cousin. The next thing you know we invited them in and they were drinking with us. Well we dated for a while and then decided it would be a good thing to get married. So we did. For a while she tried to drink with me but that was an exercise in futility. We moved around a lot, finally buying a house in order to settle down. Yeah, right.

Almost right from the beginning I was never home. I would go to the corner store for smokes and stumble in 12 hours later. Once right around the time we separated I went out and came home 10 days later. I had been to Los Angeles, Burbank, Malibu Beach, Hollywood, and Reno on the way back up. Drinking the whole way and thinking I was having a great time.

Anyhow, before all that happened, on August 12th, 1984 my wife gave birth to my son. He is such a wonderful kid; straight A's thru school, goes to university now and is possibly going into medicine. Today he and I have a great loving relationship. Fortunately and thanks to his mother he has never seen me drunk. You know, talk about a higher power intervening. I was always drinking and the weekends were especially bad. For some reason the Saturday night my wife went into labor I hadn't had a drink all day. I was able to drive her to the hospital and be there for my son's birth. The sad thing is I remember very little of the first year of my son's life. Never being home and being drunk when I was saw to that.

On my son's first birthday my wife had had enough of my selfish ways and me. She left me and took Shane. My first thought was finally, now I can drink in peace. That feeling soon became one of depression and despair. I was drinking more than ever to cover the additional pain of her leaving me. I went to the doctor and told him I was coming unglued. My nerves were shot, I drank alone a lot, and I was becoming increasingly depressed. He gave me a prescription for anti-depressants and tranquilizers. You know the kind where the label says do not take with alcohol. Well one night I was half way into a 40-ounce bottle of whiskey when I decided I wasn't going to live anymore. I was going to show my wife that she could not do this to me. I opened both bottles of pills and began taking them one at a time, washing them down with whiskey.

I don't remember how many pills I took but the last thing I remember I phoned my dad and said, "get me to the hospital, I don't want to die". The doctor said I came awfully close to doing exactly that. I was unconscious by the time I got to the hospital; my heart and lungs had stopped for a brief period of time. I now believe that more than a suicide attempt, this was a cry for help. Without my knowledge the help was soon to arrive. I just never expected the help to come in the form that it did.

As a young guy growing up I had a best friend that I used to drink with and get in trouble with all the time. His mother was in Alcoholics Anonymous. I remember that as kids we would be sitting in her basement getting drunk and she would be walking out the door going to a meeting. She would often say to us "one day you will understand why these meetings are so important to me". After the botched suicide attempt I was in the hospital for about 10 days. I remember my friends mother coming in my hospital room and saying to me "come with me, I have some friends I want you to meet". So off I go with her, dragging the IV pole that was attached to my arm and wearing the heart monitor that was around my neck.

We went upstairs into this room. It was filled with all kinds of people. They were happy. They shook my hand and said they were glad to see me. Some of them hugged me. I sat down and was amazed at the stories I heard. These people were like me. They did a lot of the things I had done. They felt a lot of the things I felt. After the meeting they told me to come back. Not many people ever asked me back anywhere. I finally felt like I belonged. I would like to mention that this best friend I speak of is now in a wheelchair after getting a ride from a drunk driver who crashed his car.

I was in the right place, the people in Alcoholics Anonymous had my heart right from that point forward, but I was far from done. One week after I got out of the hospital Alcoholics Anonymous was sponsoring a round up close to where I lived. Some AA members picked me up and put me in charge of making coffee all weekend. (A round up is a weekend long event that includes meetings, dinners, dances, and lots of fellowship with other recovering alcoholics). There is lots of fun to be had in sobriety; however, when you are young it is hard to appreciate that.

I'll never forget the kindness shown to me by the people in AA during my early sobriety. One was my friend's mother who took me to my first meeting. There are the old-timers who took me under their wings and tried to show me that I could live without alcohol. These fine people devoted a good portion of their lives to giving back to others what was so freely given to them. One does not go into a fellowship like Alcoholics Anonymous because their life is going well and is all rosy. By the time someone gets to the doors of A.A. they are usually terrified, terrified of what alcohol is doing to them and terrified of living without alcohol. Talk about being between a rock and a hard place.

After my first meeting I stayed sober for about three months. I went to a lot of meetings during that period. Once I began feeling better though that stinking thinking would kick in. I would start thinking "I'm too young for this, what am I going to do on my birthday, what am I going to do at Christmas, what am I going to do next weekend, what will my friends think". That thinking combined with the guilt I was wracked with for not being with my son soon took me back to drinking. It was the only way I knew how to cope with what was going on inside of me.

A person can come up with hundreds of reasons to go back drinking. The truth is I couldn't stand who I had become. How did my life wind up like this? Drink was the only thing that took the pain and fear away. It becomes a viscous cycle though. I drank to alleviate the pain I felt. When drinking I would do things that would just compound my shame. The next day I would have to drink because I couldn't stand myself. I also had a terrible fear of financial insecurity. Yet when I would get paid I would spend any available money on drinking and partying.

When I would leave A.A. and go back drinking my life would be okay again for a while. I was back in my element, my comfort zone. I did a lot of bar drinking. I loved everything about the bar. The dim lights, the booze soaked carpets, and the rancid smelling air. The raunchier the bar the more I liked it. At least then I could look at the guy in the corner who is sitting in his own urine and say, "hey I'm not that bad, if I ever get that bad I'll quit". I did get that bad on several occasions, yet I never quit drinking. After awhile when things got really out of control I would drag myself back into AA. The old timers would just smile, give me a hug, and say good to see you, stick around it gets better.

Even after the experience I previously had with pills and almost losing my life, whenever I quit drinking I would turn to tranquilizers to help keep me together. My doctor had some concern about this but I could be pretty convincing. It did not take long until I was addicted to the tranquilizers, specifically Xanax. I was using the pills just like alcohol, only instead of pouring a drink I would reach for the pill bottle. My body became so used to functioning on the Xanax that whenever I would attempt to go off them I would go into heavy withdrawal. My heart would feel like it was going to leap right out of my chest, I would sweat profusely, and tremble and shake. The mental anguish was probably the worst part. I wound up checking into a Detox Centre in order to help me kick the pill habit, which

I did, at least for awhile.

On one of my drinking sprees I met wife number three. We were drinking at the same bar. She was sitting there crying and I came to her rescue. That's what I did. I rescued people. That is one of the things that put me into bankruptcy. I used to think that if I came to your rescue, paid off your bills and took care of you, I would become indispensable. That way you wouldn't leave me. Not true, no one is indispensable. I found that out time and time again. I took on so much debt that I wound up filing for bankruptcy. That is all over now and I have since restored my credit. About one month after wife number three and I met we moved in together. Shortly after that we got married. I was so ashamed of what I was doing. Inside I knew I shouldn't be marrying again, but it was only one of two ways I could feel better about myself. One way was to drink myself into oblivion, and the other was to be in a relationship proving myself as a man.

I was still in my old hometown and working for the Utility Company. Now I had a ready-made family that came with two-step children. The added responsibility contributed to my drinking more and more. That and my heart still ached to be with my son. At this time I was seeing him about once per month.

I only drank with certain people because your so-called social drinkers didn't really want much to do with me. We alcoholics and addicts seek out like-minded people. We are drawn to other alcoholics and addicts like a bee to honey. I remember one of the many times my wife and I moved, friends and I were drinking all day while carrying furniture and boxes. After the move was done and evening rolled around my wife and I went to a party next door to my sisters. I was only there for a few hours when the lady of the house broke a bottle over my head just to help me on my way out the door. It seems I had gotten into a bit of a situation with her husband. I had become extremely obnoxious when drunk. I remember the next day my wife was picking the glass out of my hair as she washed the blood out of it.

Shortly after that I found myself crawling back into AA. I remember the meeting I went back to. It was a noon meeting and it was very significant for me. It was significant because this time I was really sick. I couldn't speak at that meeting for fear I would get sick if I opened my mouth. I was also very afraid for my mental and emotional stability. However, once again the people of AA welcomed me back with open arms.

I was trying hard to stay sober but it was so very difficult. I was still working with a bunch of drinkers and when trying to stay sober I didn't fit anymore, wasn't part of the crew. I once heard an old timer say that if your job is interfering with you're sobriety, get out of there. Without your sobriety you won't have a job anyway. So one day I up and quit my job. You see I thought I was pretty smart and it suddenly dawned on me that perhaps alcohol was not the problem. Perhaps the problem was the location I was living and working in.

That's it, if I get out of here and away from everyone I knew and drank with I'd be all right. So I took a job over the phone in another town, far away from everyone and everything I thought was the problem. We loaded everything we had in a 5-ton truck and off we went. I had also arranged an apartment over the phone and we moved right in. Well things started going sideways shortly after we arrived in town. The job I had taken over the phone did not work out. We then landed a job managing a motel. I stayed sober on my own for a period of time then one day I was feeling particularly cocky and figured I have this under control now, a few beers won't hurt. Besides, the Motel we managed was right next door to a pub. How convenient. Guess what, moving away didn't solve my problem. I was the problem and somehow I always wound up wherever I went. So forget about the geographical cure, doesn't work, at least it didn't for me.

I managed to keep my drinking somewhat under control for a short period of time. We quit working at the motel and took over managing a large campground and RV park. I had become well respected in that town in a short period of time. I was a member of the Chamber of Commerce, the local realtor wanted me to get my license, and the hardware store wanted me to go into sales for them.

I was even friends with the mayor and had dinner with him and his wife on several occasions. I was very good at putting on a false front, meanwhile I was full of shame and guilt, still carried the fear I always lived with, and my self esteem was in the basement. Yet the front I put on was one of confidence, strength, and courage. What a contradiction between what I portrayed on the outside and what I lived with on a daily basis on the inside. As I was so well known in town I even began driving 2 hours to go to different liquor stores so the people in my town did not know how much I was buying.

It wasn't long until my drinking was out of control again. The Campground and RV Park was a perfect place to drink while you were working. I always had a drink on the go. People would come in to camp. If they were drinkers I was right there with them. I managed to pull it off for quite a period of time. However, the time came when the alcohol wasn't working anymore. I had become unpredictable. One night I could drink a whole bottle of rye and talk as normal as could be, have fun, and not get really falling down drunk. The next night, two drinks and I was a babbling idiot. I felt I was going crazy. At one point I insisted my family physician send me to a doctor who specializes in brain disorders. The specialist did all these tests and the result was that I was fine. No brain disorder. Now I was really screwed. Now what do I blame my erratic drinking and behavior on.

My family physician was young and I believe he really cared. After awhile I had learned how to convince doctors I needed medication. I had my doctor convinced. This is when I became addicted to prescription drugs once again. Librium and Xanax were my favorites. On occasion I would even phone my doctor at home. He would meet me at the clinic in the middle of the night and give me enough Librium to ward off the DT's. I popped a lot of pills back then. Eventually I built up a tolerance to the pills as well. I would need more and more tranquilizers to calm my mind when I thought I was losing it.

After a particularly good RV season my wife and I got a nice bonus so we flew to Reno for a holiday. Free booze, ya. I drank with both fists for 4 days. I also had a half-gallon in my room for when I was there and the tranquilizers to take the edge off. On the flight home I was too sick to drink. I was falling apart. After our plane touched down I drove my wife home and then went straight to the local hospital. They kept me for a few days and then sent me to a psychiatric ward. I spent ten days there shaking and thinking I was losing my mind.

When I eventually dried out and left the psych ward I returned home. My wife insisted that I go to see this alcohol and drug counselor she had heard of. I made an appointment and went to see him, he told me what I already knew. That I was an alcoholic, I couldn't drink and I had to get back to meetings. I went home and my wife asked; "well, what did he say"? I looked her in the eye and said with a straight face, "he told me that if I only drink beer I'll be alright". You see, I had already come to the conclusion that this is what I do. I drink and I'll drink until I die. I had also become a compulsive liar. I believed my own lies half the time.

As usual the day eventually came when I was back on the phone asking for someone from AA to come see me. The guy I was talking to asked me if I was drinking now. I said no. He asked me if I thought I could stay sober till that night. I told him I thought I could. He didn't wait for the meeting time to come over. I had no sooner poured a drink and there was a knock on the door. This guy was standing there. He was older than dirt. He told me his name was Bill and he was from AA. I don't remember exactly what happened next but I know I went to a meeting with him that night.

Bill turned out to be a great friend. We used to call him Doctor Bill because at one time he was the only dentist in town. Dr. Bill, the drunken dentist. I remember a friend telling me that one night he had a terrible toothache. He called doctor Bill who met him at the office. Bill kept a piano in the back room and usually had a bottle sitting on top of it. My friend said he could see every once in awhile that old Bill would go in the back and have a swig out of the bottle. He froze my friends jaw, went in the back and took a pull from the bottle, came out and started yanking on the wrong tooth. Jack said the dentist almost needed a doctor. After awhile Bill lost his dental practice because of his drinking. After he got sober he took on three jobs. This was at 60 years of age. He was the dogcatcher, the sheriff, and the jailer.

He was a great man. I was slipping again in the beginning but Bill wouldn't give up. He was like a tree in the backyard, always there. Bill's heart was certainly in the right place. He always wanted to help me stay sober. As I look back on it Bill played a big part in saving my life. Soon after this I went into a treatment center. I spent 28 days there. When I went to treatment I almost didn't get off the bus I was so scared. The treatment center was a fabulous experience but I was still a mess on the inside. I spent Christmas of 1990 in that treatment center. After I got out of there I went home and began going to AA again. I remember not wanting to go to the treatment center because being a small town everyone would know I was an alcoholic and would think less of me. The exact opposite turned out to be true. They all knew how I drank and were just glad to see I was trying to do something about it.

When I got home from the treatment center people who I didn't even think knew I drank came up to me and said stuff like, "hey, I hear you quit drinking, good for you, you know you were a real ***** ***** when you drank." So don't ever be embarrassed about trying to do something positive for yourself. You weren't embarrassed before when you stumbling around stinking of booze, why should you be embarrassed when you are trying to help yourself?

About one month after I got out of the treatment center I had to go on a road trip in order to purchase some machinery for the company I was working for. I noticed every liquor store in every town on my way there. I realize now I was setting myself up the whole way, looking for an excuse to drink. I thought about my son, the mistakes I had made, generally feeling really sorry for myself. When I got there, I did my business and then went and picked a motel that had a bar on one side and a cabaret on the other. I came home three days later. Now, why on earth after being through what I had been through would I go back drinking like that? I believe I know why. I hadn't surrendered to the fact that I was an alcoholic. That and the pain I was living with inside was incredible. After five years of AA, detox, and a treatment center I was still looking for any means at all that would block the shame, guilt, pain, and remorse that I carried with me.

I arrived back home and went to a friend's house. I sat at her kitchen table and cried like a baby. She took me to a meeting that night and they were talking about honesty. I cried through most of that meeting as well. That was the last time I ever took a drink. That was also the last time I abused prescription drugs, or for that matter, any kind of drug. As of this coming February 28th, 2005, I will have been clean and sober for 13 years.

My sobriety has been a difficult one. I went through another divorce shortly after I became sober. I went from living in a house on a lake, all my bills paid by the company I worked for, to living in a beat up Motel room, all I had was my duffle bag. I did some nasty things up there when I was drinking. I had an old gravel truck and a backhoe. My job was to haul fill into the property where the RV Park was. We were raising the whole place by about 5 feet and leveling it out. I would haul fill all week. The company was paying for it by the truckload. Then come the weekend I would put a couple of loads back on the truck and sell it elsewhere. All this to get some extra cash to support my drinking habit. An old timer in AA told me I had to go to any lengths if I wanted to remain sober and that including making amends to the boss I had been stealing gravel from. I expected to pay it back but he said he appreciated my coming forward and not to worry about it. I was amazed. He just wanted me to get well. I eventually left that job, as it was time to move on.

The difficulty with my sobriety was that I wasn't drinking, but that is all I had changed. I kept on doing a lot of the things I used to do when I was an active alcoholic. And for the life of me I could not understand why, either could anyone else. I was not drinking but I lived on a daily basis with this terrible ache inside. At times I still did not want to live. However, I persevered, I stayed sober. The people in AA kept me sober. You often hear that you have to work the twelve steps right away if you want to stay sober. Personally I don't believe that. It was all I could do to keep from killing myself let alone work the twelve steps. So I stayed sober on the fellowship, the meetings, and the love of the people, even if I didn't think I was worthy. The first year I was sober I was at a meeting almost every night.

You see when you take the booze out of your life you are left with this huge void. You have to fill that void in a healthy manner or you are headed for trouble. I filled it with the people of Alcoholics Anonymous.

I did a lot of things wrong the first year I was sober. They told me to get a male sponsor. I found a female one. Six months later we were living together. My old behaviors stuck with me. I was still desperately trying to mask my pain. I was on thin ice and I knew it. There was many times during my sobriety that I felt I was going crazy. That is because there was a direct conflict between what I knew was right and my behavior. Today I look at what is important to me and I check to see if my behavior reflects my values. I can honestly say that today it does.

A lot of very positive things happened during the first five years of my sobriety. I only had a grade ten education so after my first year of sobriety I wrote the GED test and received my grade twelve equivalency. I then began applying to different colleges and universities. I was accepted into a University that was near my old hometown. Now here is an example of when you try to do the right things, the right things happen. Remember my son? His Mother in her wisdom left me when he was one year old. I then didn't see too much of him for the next 6 years.

Well, now I'm sober and moving to a new town in order to continue my education. Without my knowing it my son and his mother moved to the same town one month before I did. My son and I were able to rekindle our relationship and today we are closer than ever. I see him all the time. He comes to my place whenever he can. He loves me and he tells me that often. Now he is off to University himself. I am very proud of him.

Shortly after I changed locations in order to continue my education my next oldest sister approached me. I will never forget the look on her face. She had a black eye and was crying. She had passed out when drunk and hit her head on the corner of the coffee table. She told me that she was in trouble. She couldn't stop drinking. She needed help. I was able to stay with her and get her the help she needed. She has flourished in sobriety and is a beautiful person. Now she is sober she has been able to carry the message to my cousin who has also been able to put the drinking behind her. I am very proud of both of them. Many people may disagree with me, but I believe that alcoholism and addiction has a genetic component to it and it can run in families.

I graduated from University with two associate degrees, one in Social Services and the other in Substance Abuse Counseling. Through a series of events I began working with incarcerated men as a program facilitator/substance abuse counselor. There is nothing I can think of that I would rather do. I am now making a living working in a field that I love, trying to help men turn their lives around. It is challenging work, it can be frustrating, but I have seen some men make drastic changes in their lives. That is what makes it worthwhile.

So I now had a great career, I was sober, but my biggest problem was still the fact that my emotional health was not very good. There were times when I would get on my knees, look up at the sky and say someone, anyone, please help me. I was still bouncing in and out of relationships, doing what I did when drinking, only now doing it sober. I was in a lot of pain inside. I was sober about six years when my Father was put in the hospital. Between his alcoholism and the emphysema he suffered with, we knew that when he went in the hospital he wouldn't be coming out.

I drove my father to the hospital one Saturday. I believe he knew he would not be coming home. I had to pour him a double whiskey before he would leave with me. While he was in the hospital he kept trying to introduce me to his nurse who he had discovered was single. I kept saying no, that I was busy but he wouldn't let up. Finally I asked her out for coffee which turned into dinner which turned into another marriage. When I look back on it now it seems like a dream. I knew it was wrong, I cried before the day of the ceremony, but I couldn't stop it. I was never so close to drinking as I was at that point. I was an emotional wreck.

For some reason I could not live with myself. I still had to have someone or something to divert my attention. I think the marriage was doomed before it started. Once again I had gotten married for the wrong reasons. The worst part was now I didn't even have alcohol to blame it on. Rather I had a secret inside that was soon to be revealed, one that I wasn't even aware of. It is that secret that kept me living in fear and doing everything in my power to escape myself. That marriage lasted four months. It happened, it's over. I was so full of shame and disgust around the things I had done and the things I was still doing. From my eyes things looked pretty bleak. I would like to take this opportunity to apologize to anyone who has endured the whirlwind that has been portions of my past.

The only thing that really kept my sanity was my work and AA. I could throw myself into either one of those and forget for a brief period of time. With the work I now do and a busy family life I don't get to many AA meetings anymore. But believe me when I tell you that in my early sobriety it was AA that saved my life and I am grateful for that to this day. Still I knew I needed outside help and I was willing to do anything at this point. I called this number out of the phone book and I was hooked up with who I believe was the one special person that could help me.

I began seeing a local Psychologist. She is a wonderful woman. Often let me come to my own conclusions. She knew something was horribly wrong with me on the inside. It took two years and many tears to finally get to what it was that was destroying my life. One day during an appointment we came to the conclusion that I did not like myself. In fact, I hated myself. Everything I had ever done was done to ensure my discomfort, despair, unhappiness, and to make sure I punished my self sufficiently. That day I cried in her office for a solid hour. I now knew that I had despised myself and for many years had regretted every breath I drew. I cried and cried still not knowing what was wrong. Was I really crazy? I had despised myself for most of my life and I did everything I could to harm myself through alcoholism, addiction, hurtful and harmful relationships, and other destructive behavior.

I left my therapists office and went to a very dear friend's house for dinner. I credit her with being the catalyst that helped me to break through a lifetime of forgotten memories. She asked me how my therapy session went and I burst into tears. The next words out of her mouth have altered my life forever. I will never forget the question she asked me. She looked at me and said, "Who hurt you"? Three little words and all the memories came flooding back.

The memories of the sexual abuse I suffered as a young child. I know whom, I know where, I know when, but I do not remember any details. Our mind only gives us what we can handle. It took about 37 years for these memories to come back. Maybe I will never get any more memories but that's okay. After months of journaling and seeing my therapist my life now makes sense. I now have answers.

I now know why I did so many of the things I did. I don't have to be ashamed anymore of the things I have done. I lived my whole life in fear up until these memories came. I had fear of people in authority over me, fear of not being able to make it on my own, fear of financial insecurity.

I have spoken to others who are recovering from the effects of childhood sexual abuse. Our stories are almost identical. All the pieces are there: the alcoholism, the drug addiction, the multiple marriages, and the demand for relationships. The effects of this type of abuse contributed to my declaring bankruptcy. I was trying to buy my way out of the feelings I felt. The effects of this type of abuse are devastating. I wonder if the abusers of the world knew what they were doing to us, would they stop? Doubtful, that type of sick behavior is all about power, control, and getting selfish needs met at the expense of others.

Everything I did to try and destroy myself up to this point is all tied to this horrific act that was perpetrated against me as a child. But guess what, it's okay. It's okay because I'm still sober, it's okay because my life now makes sense, and it's okay because I am getting to the point where I no longer live in fear. It's okay because I now know that I am going to be alright, and I am getting to the point where I can truly love another, not for the sex or what they can offer me, but for who they are inside as a person.

I have been angry, so angry that I wanted to drive to where I could confront the person that abused me. I still may, but not until I get to the point where I don't want him harmed, if I ever do. I still feel that way. It is okay to feel it but I still do not know if I trust myself enough to not to act on it. Today I am strong. Today I am confident. Today I know I am perfect just the way I am.

Let me tell you, I am very grateful to be alive today. Each day is an experience to be cherished, a chance to do something for someone else, and a chance at life. So let us see. How did I get to where I am and how did I begin the process of recovery?

- For many years all I did is cope any way I could. Alcohol, drugs, moving around, relationships, all these things were in place to mask the pain I felt inside. I know I would not have survived otherwise.

- I had to become willing to allow people in AA to love me, even when I could not love myself.

- I had to be strong enough to recognize when I needed help and not be afraid to ask for it.

- I had to believe in spirituality. I always believed I was destined for something greater.

- I had to admit that alcohol had me beat and that I was an alcoholic.

- I had to be willing to go to any lengths to stay sober, whether that meant quitting a job or leaving a relationship.

- I had to go for outside help. My therapist has been a godsend. Without her I do not think I ever would have broken the barrier surrounding the sexual abuse I suffered as a child. That had to be opened in order for me to heal.

- I continue to work with others that suffer from alcoholism or drug addiction. If it had not been for the old timers who carried the message of sobriety to me I would probably not be here writing this.

It has been a long painful journey that is far from over. Today I love life. I am free, I am confident, I am worthy, and above all I am grateful. My past is still painful but it is just that, my past. Today I am moving forward. Forward into a future that is full of hope and many new experiences.

One other thing, I guess to wrap this up I would like to tell you about my friend Holly. She was a good friend of mine. I met her at work. We often had lunch together and she would come and confide in me when she was struggling. We had lunch together on Friday July 4th, 2003 .We both left work at the same time that afternoon. She was going on holidays the next day and I told her to enjoy herself and that I would see her when she got back to work. That day when Holly and I parted company in the parking lot it never crossed my mind that I would never see her again. She was killed in a car accident the next day.

Why I brought this up now is simple. In the last few pages I have told you about my alcoholism, drug addiction, and the sexual abuse that I suffered from as a child, and I told you about my friends death. There are two messages I want to get across really clearly and here they are.

1. Try not to judge people by their actions for you have no idea what is lurking beneath the surface. People are individuals and were put on this earth as perfect beings. Somehow, something or someone discolored the perfect canvas that they were at birth. Perhaps they have no idea what is behind their actions. I know some people commit such heinous acts that we cannot or perhaps should not forgive them. I am talking more about family, friends, everyday people, and others in recovery.

2. Be kind to each other, life is so fragile. My friend Holly is an example of that.

Simple eh, do not judge and be kind. Easier said than done some days but I think if we give it a shot it will be a better world to live in.

Thank you for taking the time to read this. My hope is that maybe something written here triggered something within you that will be either helpful for you or someone else. So, let's get started on your recovery and if you are ready we will move onto the workbook.

Sincerely,

Steve Lloyd

This self-help program is written in a way that is easy for all to understand. Take your time as you work through it. Think about what you are reading and the answers you are giving. If you have the benefit of having a spouse or someone close to you who is willing, get them to provide their insight to some of the questions. This can help immensely when we get someone else's perspective. It can help us to see things we may have otherwise overlooked.

The C.A.R.E. program is not meant to replace professional counseling or therapy. It is not meant to be a substitute for the human interaction that support groups provide. Rather it is meant to be a foundation for positive personal growth and to compliment other sources of help that are available. On the other hand, this program may be all you need to gain enough insight into your problem so that you can begin to move forward while living a clean and sober lifestyle.

You may find that you acquire enough knowledge and recovery based skills to move on with your life and never look back. We must remember that we are all individuals. What works well for one may not be the answer for another. Whatever this program does for you, take it, run with it, and don't be afraid to begin your new life of freedom from the bonds of addiction and alcoholism. Good luck and stick with it. Rome wasn't built in a day, and recovery doesn't happen in an afternoon. It is work, but it is work you will never regret doing.

CHAPTER 1

DEFINITIONS/WHAT CAUSES ADDICTION

COMBATING ADDICTION THROUGH RECOVERY EDUCATION

THE C.A.R.E. PROGRAM

DEFINITIONS/WHAT CAUSES ADDICTION

Welcome to the beginning of the journey. First of all it is necessary to understand that alcoholism and drug addiction does not discriminate when it comes to destroying lives. Anyone can become afflicted with the condition of chemical dependency. People from doctors and lawyers to housewives and teenagers are susceptible to the destruction caused by substance use/abuse. For that reason this workbook is written in a format that all can understand and hopefully benefit from. So as not to cause any confusion, from here forward I will be referring to alcoholism and drug addiction as chemical dependency. Once a substance has begun to control you the name we give it is not as important as what we are going to do about the situation.

I need you to know that you can be successful in overcoming your difficulties. However, it is going to take work on your part. You have got to want to change your life and you must be willing to put as much effort into your recovery as you put into using your substance of choice. We are going to begin by defining some basic terms.

DEFINITION – ADDICTION

Addiction/Chemical Dependency/Alcoholism it does not matter what you call it, the below definition applies to all.

Addiction is the compulsive use of a drug and/or alcohol at an increasing dose and frequency, despite the serious physical and psychological consequences caused by the use and the severe disruption of the users relationships, values, and life areas.

WHAT CAUSES PEOPLE TO BECOME ADDICTED?

There are several theories as to how people become addicted. The most common theory and the one that this I subscribes to is:
THE *BIO-PSYCHO-SOCIAL* MODEL OF ADDICTION

The BIO-PSYCHO-SOCIAL MODEL IS A 3 PART THEORY

1. **Biological,** meaning that addiction/alcoholism may be hereditary and passed from one generation to the next. You may have a personal predisposition to addiction/alcoholism.

2. **Psychological**, we think we need the drink/drug. The drink or drug may help us to cope, it becomes our crutch and we become psychologically dependent.

3. **Social Learning,** a very influential and core component of addiction.
People learn at a young age what is acceptable and what is not.
If you are raised with the belief that drinking/drugging is acceptable
then you are more apt to partake in substance use/abuse yourself.

Any one of these three items above or a combination of all of them can cause the onset of addiction.

No matter what theory one prescribes to, the bottom line is that addiction is a major problem and needs to be dealt with. That is what the rest of this workbook is about. Making one's life more manageable and enjoyable without having to partake in drinking or drugging.

DEFINITIONS

What is a drug?

Answer – A drug is any substance, other than food, which is taken to change the way the body and the mind functions. This includes alcohol, street drugs such as cocaine, heroin, marijuana, hallucinogens, and prescription drugs.

Can you think of other substances that would fall under the category, what is a drug?

_____

_____

_____

My personal drug/drink of choice has been

_____

_____

_____

What is drug/alcohol abuse?

Answer – Drug and or alcohol abuse is any use of a drug or alcohol that is problematic. As stated earlier, drug or alcohol use is problematic if it causes you problems in any of the following areas.

- family/friends/relationships
- work or school
- finances
- legal issues
- leisure time

My examples of problems caused by my drug or alcohol use are

_____

_____

_____

_____

_____

_____

_____

_____
_____
_____
_____
_____
_____

Psychological dependence – occurs when the user becomes mentally and emotionally preoccupied with the substance. The user begins to think constantly about the substance and the effect it has on them.

Physical dependence – Occurs when the body has become adapted to the substance and needs it to function properly. When the user abruptly stops using the substance the user goes into withdrawal. Depending on the substance, withdrawal ranges in severity from being uncomfortable to life threatening.

Tolerance – Tolerance is when the user needs more of the substance (higher amounts) or uses the substance more often in order to feel the same effects.

Cross tolerance – When the body and brain becomes tolerant to a substance from a specific category, it will also be tolerant to other drugs from the same category.
(i.e. alcohol, valium)

CHAPTER 2

CLASSIFICATIONS OF DRUGS

COMBATING ADDICTION THROUGH RECOVERY EDUCATION

THE C.A.R.E. PROGRAM

CLASSIFICATIONS OF DRUGS

All drugs either speed up or slow down your central nervous system. The central nervous system is the spine and brain, it controls everything we do. Listed below are the five main categories of drugs and examples of each.

Depressants – e.g. alcohol, heroin, tranquilizers
Stimulants – e.g. cocaine, speed, crystal methamphetamine
Hallucinogens – e.g. LSD, PCP, magic mushrooms, marijuana
Inhalants – e.g. aerosol sprays, gasoline, glue
Pharmaceuticals – e.g. prescribed medications, over the counter medication

CHAPTER 3

THE EARLY GOING/ GETTING MEDICAL HELP

COMBATING ADDICTION THROUGH RECOVERY EDUCATION

THE C.A.R.E. PROGRAM

GETTING MEDICAL HELP IN THE EARLY GOING

It is not uncommon for a person to become addicted to one or more of the above-mentioned substances. Something that happens far too often is that an alcoholic will go to his or her doctor seeking relief from the misery caused by their drinking. They will complain of suffering from anxiety, confused thinking, and not sleeping well. The doctor may ask them how much they drink. Of course the answer is "not much, maybe one or two per week" (alcoholics are anything but honest). So the doctor may prescribe a tranquilizer of some sort to help ease the patient's discomfort. As alcohol and tranquilizers are both central nervous system depressants and the patient has become used to the effects of depressants, we have the birth of another addiction. I know this to be fact as it happened to me. The doctor who was trying to help unknowingly created another monster that became right out of control.

The combination of tranquilizers and alcohol put me in the hospital, once almost taking my life. I highly recommend that if you feel you have a drug and or alcohol problem you make an appointment to see your physician as soon as possible. The key here is to be **HONEST.** Tell your physician about your substance use. Tell him or her everything including what you have been using and for how long. Tell the good doctor what you are trying to do and ask for his/her support. You will be amazed how supportive your doctor will be. If you are completely honest your physician will be able to help you in ways that are not going to compound your problem.

Am I willing to make a doctor's appointment? _____

Am I willing to be completely honest with my doctor? _____

Physician's name _____

Physician' phone number _____

Physicians address _____

Date and time of appointment _____

Do I need to take a supportive person with me, if so, who? _____

In many big centers there are doctors who specialize in treating chemical dependency. If you can you may prefer to seek out one of these. If not a family physician can be very effective in helping you in the early stages of your recovery.

Some other tips that are helpful in the early going are:

- Eat properly, a balanced diet is best
- Take a multi vitamin on a daily basis; your body has likely been depleted of essential nutrients for some time.
- Mild exercise such as walking
- Drink plenty of water and juices
- Get enough rest
- Try not to isolate yourself. You need people. If you have family around you, tell them what you are trying to do and ask for their support.

Now I would like to share with you some of the harmful effects of a few of the more popular substances that people become dependent on. By no measure is this a complete inventory of all the harmful affects substance abuse can have. Nor is it a complete list of all the drugs that people become dependent on. If you are concerned in any way about your health, consult your physician as soon as possible. If you require more information on a specific drug the Internet or library are both great resources.

CHAPTER 4

HARMFUL EFFECTS OF ALCOHOL/HEROIN/ COCAINE AND MARIJUANA

COMBATING ADDICTION THROUGH RECOVERY EDUCATION

THE C.A.R.E. PROGRAM

HARMFUL EFFECTS OF ALCOHOL/HEROIN/COCAINE/ AND MARIJUANA

HARMFUL EFFECTS OF ALCOHOL

Alcoholism is chronic condition that usually starts out as a harmless way of socializing. However, for a percentage of people, what starts out as relaxing and fun soon turns into an uncontrollable destroyer of lives. Alcoholism tears families apart, ends careers, causes mental and emotional breakdowns, crushes one's spirit, and is a very lonely condition to live with. The person afflicted has a reduced level of inhibitions often resulting in high-risk behaviors that can lead to injury or death. Many people in our society drink alcohol moderately and experience no problems. However, there is a segment of our society whose alcohol use ties up hospital emergency rooms, causes inflated health care costs, keeps the coroner's office busy, fragments families, and causes numerous other tragedies.

Withdrawal from alcohol is a serious condition that often follows periods of heavy drinking. It usually begins during the 24 hours after the last drink and may persist for up to 5 to 7 days. Symptoms include nausea, shaking, sweating, increased heart rate, high blood pressure, and severe anxiety. Hallucinations often accompany severe withdrawal. The DT's are not uncommon. I have personally known people who have destroyed their surrounding because they were convinced they saw snakes, or some other hallucination during the DT's. Fatal heart attacks can occur when experiencing delirium tremens. .

Depression is another effect of heavy alcohol consumption. This has been known to lead to suicide amongst alcoholics. Unless the person affected has a medical disorder, the depression should lift after a period of abstinence.

A major concern for alcoholics is that prolonged drinking over a substantial period of time can result in what is known as "wet brain," or Korsakoff's syndrome. The result of which can resemble someone who has had a stroke. Short-term memory is inhibited and patients often wind up being institutionalized.

There are many more harmful effects of prolonged heavy alcohol consumption. A partial list includes: liver disease, high blood pressure, accidents, trauma, infertility, and death.

HARMFUL EFFECTS OF HEROIN

Heroin is a highly addictive drug. Tolerance to the drug develops quickly resulting in the user having to use a larger dose and more often in order to achieve the effect they are looking for. Heroin belongs to the drug category Central Nervous System Depressant. Heroin overdose is a very real risk on the street as it is difficult to gauge the purity of the drug. People often cut the drug with other substances to make it go further.

Once addicted the user will go to extreme measures to ensure the supply of heroin is available. Withdrawal from heroin is very uncomfortable and can come on rapidly after the last use. This is why the addict's main focus in life becomes the acquiring and using of heroin. Everything else becomes secondary, including family, health, work, school, and life itself. Short-term effects of heroin use include but are not limited to slowed respiration, clouded mental ability, nausea, and vomiting. Long-term effects include severe infections (heart lining and valves), skin abscesses, collapsed veins, and diseases such as HIV/AIDS, hepatitis C and others. Heroin overdose can produce coma and death.

The principle cause of death from heroin overdose is respiratory arrest as heroin slows the portion of the brain that controls breathing.

The most common methods of using heroin are:

- Intravenous injection (mainlining)
- Snorting
- Skin popping (injecting just under the skin)
- Smoking (chasing the dragon)

Heroin users often turn to crime to support their habit placing a huge social burden on society. Whether direct or indirect, involvement with heroin is a huge contributor to the population of incarcerated male offenders.

HARMFUL EFFECTS OF COCAINE

Cocaine belongs to the drug category Central Nervous System Stimulant. Addiction to cocaine can happen very rapidly and its use often results in tragedy. Cocaine is such a powerful stimulant that the addiction can be hard to break. The high from cocaine is not long lasting but the resulting depression after coming down can be overwhelming, resulting in the addict going to extreme measures to obtain more cocaine. Intense psychological dependence causes powerful cravings that can be triggered even after a long period of abstinence. This can happen simply by being reminded of something associated with cocaine use. Users who continue to use despite obvious harmful evidence show how powerful cocaine dependence is. Cocaine is a very dangerous drug and the effects can be life threatening.

Methods of use:

Cocaine hydrochloride (powdered cocaine)

- Snorting into nose
- Injecting intravenously

ROCK OR CRACK

- This cocaine has been rendered down, must be smoked

Sudden death from cocaine use is fairly common. It is usually the result of an irregular heartbeat, cocaine induced seizures, bleeding in the brain, or respiratory arrest. When a person dies from cocaine overdose death happens so rapidly that there is usually not enough time for medical help to respond.

Cocaine induced strokes are the result of an increase in blood pressure brought on by cocaine combined with a weak blood vessel in the brain. This can be compared to turning on a garden hose at full pressure while having the sprayer at the far end of the hose turned off. If there is a weak spot in the garden hose, the pressure of the water will eventually blow a hole through the side of the hose. The same can happen with the blood vessels in your brain.

Intravenous injection of cocaine brings about the same dangers found with injecting any drug. You run the risk of catching diseases such as HIV, Hepatitis, and skin abscesses.

Withdrawal brings on severe depression (the cocaine crash) at times making the user suicidal. Other withdrawal symptoms include:

- Paranoia
- Irritability
- Mental confusion
- Memory loss

Cocaine is a very powerful and addictive drug, it has been compared to a miraculous thief as it steals from a person:

- their self esteem
- their family
- financial independence
- employment
- capacity to love
- morals
- values
- sense of self-worth

HARMFUL EFFECTS OF MARIJUANA

Marijuana belongs to the hallucinogenic category of drugs. It is a Central Nervous System depressant. Marijuana is still one of the most controversial of the illicit drugs. Although marijuana is one of the less dangerous drugs, this does not mean it does not have many harmful effects.

At low to moderate doses it can cause; increased heart rate, muscle weakness, mild impairment of coordination, slight tremors, reddened eyes, involuntary movement of the eyeballs, slightly increased body temperature, increased appetite and dry mouth. At higher doses marijuana can cause severe anxiety, panic reactions, paranoid thinking, and frightening hallucinations.

All drugs are either fat-soluble or water-soluble. The THC within marijuana is fat soluble, meaning it clings to the fat cells within your body. For this reason marijuana stays in your system for a long period of time (up to 30 days after smoking one joint). Brain cells are encased in a thin cushion of fat cells. The THC in marijuana clings to these cells and builds up over time, thus impairing the brain cells from working properly. This can bring on what is called A MOTIVATIONAL SYNDROME. This syndrome is evident in that the user feels listless, has no energy, no ambition, and no drive.

The task of convincing a marijuana user of the harmful effects of its use is very difficult. People do not associate marijuana use with major crime, overdose, or other harmful effects. From my point of view the bottom line is this. Marijuana is still illegal; it changes the way the body and mind functions, and no matter what you may think does have harmful effects. If you are going to be clean and sober, why not be really clean and sober. How do you know what it is like on the other side of the fence until you have been over there?

HARMFUL EFFECTS OF ECSTACY

Ecstasy is a drug that has become very popular amongst the younger generation. Users of ecstasy often frequent the rave scene. Raves are all night dance parties where people dance, hug, and proclaim their connectedness and love toward one another. This loss of inhibition is a side affect of the drug and is the reason why it was given the nickname of the "love drug" or "hug drug".

Ecstasy produces an increased need for interpersonal relationships and users report a strong desire to be with others. Users of Ecstasy risk many of the same effects that cocaine users face. Heart rhythm abnormalities, increased blood pressure, faintness, and involuntary teeth clenching are some of the common symptoms of ecstasy use.

The most common cause of ecstasy related death is overheating (hyperthermia). When on ecstasy the body's ability to regulate its temperature is interfered with. The body can overheat without displaying the normal warning signs. When the drug wears of the user is normally left feeling exhausted and may suffer from extreme anxiety.

CHAPTER 5

DECISIONAL BALANCE/ PERSONAL EXERCISE

COMBATING ADDICTION THROUGH RECOVERY EDUCATION

THE C.A.R.E. PROGRAM

DECISIONAL BALANCE/ PERSONAL EXERCISE

INTRODUCTION TO A DECISIONAL BALANCE

Below is an example of a decisional balance on the short and long term effects of alcohol use/abuse. As you can see there are short-term positives associated with alcohol use, but compare that to the short and long term negatives effects.

Decisional balance on the use of alcohol

Short term		Long term	
Pos.	**Neg.**	**Pos.**	**Neg.**
party	fight		liver disease
happy	argue		family breakup
lose inhibit.	impaired		jail
socialize	poor judgment		wet brain
	arrest		divorce
	sick		financial ruin
	expensive		death
	accidents		loss of trust
			poor nutrition
			loss of friends
			loss of job

Now it is your turn. Do a decisional balance on the short and long term effects of the substance you use the most often.

Short Term		Long Term	
+	−	+	−
_____	_____	_____	_____
_____	_____	_____	_____
_____	_____	_____	_____
_____	_____	_____	_____
_____	_____	_____	_____
_____	_____	_____	_____
_____	_____	_____	_____
_____	_____	_____	_____

Perhaps you have known all along that you have a substance use/abuse problem, or perhaps you are just coming to that awareness now. People often spend a great deal of time in denial about their condition. Let's explore just exactly what denial is.

CHAPTER 6

WHAT IS DENIAL/ HOW TO OVERCOME IT

COMBATING ADDICTION THROUGH RECOVERY EDUCATION

THE C.A.R.E. PROGRAM

WHAT IS DENIAL?

Denial is a psychological process by which human beings protect themselves from something threatening to them by blocking knowledge of that thing from their awareness.

The denial of chemically dependent persons consists of their lack of awareness of their excessive and/or inappropriate use of substances and the resulting harmful consequences.

Denial is a core component of chemical dependency. When it comes to denial we tend to use it as if we were protecting a best friend or a lover. It is denial that permits the chemically dependent person to ignore the physician's advice of **"STOP OR YOU WILL DIE"**.

DENIAL IS AUTOMATIC

Denial in its various forms is not usually a matter of deliberate lying or willful deception. It is a serious psychological mechanism, which operates unconsciously. In most cases chemically dependent people do not know what is true or false concerning their substance use/abuse and its consequences.

DENIAL IS PROGRESSIVE

As the illness of chemical dependency progresses, denial becomes more persuasive and entrenched. By the time chemical dependency is sufficiently advanced, and the problem begins to appear serious in the eyes of others, an elaborate system of defenses shields the chemically dependent person from seeing what is really happening.

DEFENCES

DENIAL HAS MANY FACES

SIMPLE DENIAL
Maintaining that something is not so, insisting that substance use/abuse is not a problem, despite obvious evidence that it is a problem.

MINIMIZING
Making the problem out to be much less serious than it is.

BLAMING
Denying responsibility for certain behavior and maintaining that the responsibility lies somewhere or with someone else.

RATIONALIZING
Behavior is not denied, but an inaccurate explanation of its cause is given.

HOSTILITY
Becoming angry or irritable when the subject of substance use/abuse is brought up.

Which forms of denial have you engaged in? Based on the above give some examples of when you were engaging in denial.

_____
_____
_____
_____
_____
_____
_____
_____

HOW DO WE BEGIN TO OVERCOME DENIAL?

This can be described with the acronym **H.O.W.**

HONESTY - Be honest with yourself. Where has your substance use/abuse taken you in the past? What hardships have you and or your loved ones had to endure because of substance use/abuse? What makes you think it will be any different in the future if you continue to use?

Openness - Be open-minded. Could there be another way? What can I learn that can possibly help me?

Willingness - Be willing to try something new. If you don't try, you will never know what life can and will be without the use of substances.

CHAPTER 7

WHY IS SOBRIETY IMPORTANT TO ME

COMBATING ADDICTION THROUGH RECOVERY EDUCATION

THE C.A.R.E. PROGRAM

WHY SOBRIETY IS IMPORTANT TO ME

PERSONAL EXERCISE

Write down at least ten reasons why it is important to you to begin to take control of your life and escape from the bonds of chemical dependency.

1. _____
2. _____
3. _____
4. _____
5. _____
6. _____
7. _____
8. _____
9. _____
10. _____

As I mentioned earlier when telling you a little about myself, I spent five years trying to get sober. I would get two or three months in and then go back drinking. I would convince myself to go back by telling myself things like "I'm too young yet", or "What am I going to do on my birthday," "What will I do next Christmas," "life is going to be so boring," or my favorite, "I can handle it, it will be different next time."

Let me tell you every time I went back drinking things only got worse, never better. Often during the early stages of not drinking I would feel like I was going crazy. Once I went to my doctor and insisted I get my brain tested, as I was sure there was something seriously wrong. There wasn't, the only thing seriously wrong was that I was an alcoholic who for two thirds of his life had had been destroying himself with alcohol. So, what was wrong, why was I so emotionally out of control.

What I was suffering from was **Post Acute Withdrawal.** I am going to explain to you exactly what post acute withdrawal is and hopefully help alleviate some of the anxiety you may be experiencing.

CHAPTER 8

POST ACUTE WITHDRAWAL

COMBATING ADDICTION THROUGH RECOVERY EDUCATION

THE C.A.R.E. PROGRAM

POST ACUTE WITHDRAWAL

What is post acute withdrawal?

Post acute withdrawal is a compilation of symptoms that come on after the alcohol or addict has ceased using substances. The degree to which alcoholics and addicts punish their systems has detrimental effects on the brain and central nervous system. These are called neurological consequences. The symptoms are similar to someone who has had a stroke or head injury, affected are the memory, the emotions, and the intellect.

You may find that your mind begins to race. You may have repetitive thoughts over and over again and not be able to stop it. You may have trouble holding a thought for any period of time. Your judgment can seem distorted.

Despite trying very hard to remember simple things such as a phone number you may find that things just seem to disappear from memory. This is because you have an inability to transfer things from short-term memory to long-term memory.

You may find that you over react to small situations, make mountains out of molehills. A big thing is you may find yourself feeling emotions and not knowing why. You may cry for no apparent reason. You may feel you are going crazy. You may get angry for no apparent reason.

Now, that is all the unpleasant news. Are you ready for a little better stuff? Here it is and read this carefully. Post acute withdrawal is not a permanent condition. Symptoms can last from 6 months to 2 years. However by taking care of yourself and following a few simple suggestions you can lessen the effects. Your symptoms will gradually lessen until they get to the point where they are no longer bothersome.

So, here are a few tips for you. Get a thorough check up from a physician. Get regular exercise. Talk to someone about what is going on for you. A burden shared is not as heavy. Do not isolate, you need people, healthy people. Eat properly and get enough rest. Following these few tips will help you through the process.

CHAPTER 9
TRIGGERS AND HOW TO COMBAT THEM

COMBATING ADDICTION THROUGH RECOVERY EDUCATION

THE C.A.R.E. PROGRAM

TRIGGERS AND WHAT WE CAN DO ABOUT THEM

When I talk about triggers I mean people, places, and/or things that can cause a person to crave substances and develop euphoric recall.

EUPHORIC RECALL – Remembering the good times had when using substances, while at the same time ignoring the memories of the negative consequences.

A trigger may be something such as a familiar street corner where you used to buy drugs or alcohol, driving by a familiar bar, or being around someone you used to drink/use with. For myself, in my early sobriety, just going to a licensed restaurant was a trigger and resulted in my craving alcohol. I always associated going out to dinner with drinking. It is this association that causes the craving. For the first year of my sobriety I avoided licensed establishments all together. I had to if I wanted to stay sober. One of the keys to sobriety is being aware of your triggers and having a plan to deal with them when they come up. What you are going to do now is discover what your main triggers are.

ASK – When it comes to drinking alcohol or using drugs what are some examples of people, places, and things that have proven to be triggers for you? Try to come up with ten.

1. _____
2. _____
3. _____
4. _____
5. _____
6. _____
7. _____
8. _____
9. _____
10. _____

Now, from the above ten triggers pick out what you consider to be your top five.

1. _____
2. _____
3. _____
4. _____
5. _____

In order to be successful you have to find another manner of coping with your triggers when they arise. Below is an example of what a person may do when they are trying to refrain from drinking or using drugs. In this scenario I have used the example of attending a wedding. The same principle can be applied to any situation that may prove to be a high risk for you.

(UNHEALTHY MANNER OF COPING)

TRIGGER	OLD BEHAVIOUR	CONSEQUENCE
attend wedding	drink use drugs	poor judgment inappropriate behavior conflict with others/law hung over

(HEALTHY MANNER OF COPING)

TRIGGER	NEW BEHAVIOUR	REWARDS
attend wedding	go with someone who doesn't drink keep a pop in your hand do not stay for reception don't go explain to people that you don't drink	no conflict stay sober self-esteem no embarrassment pride

YOUR TOP 5 TRIGGERS AND HOW YOU CAN COPE WITH THEM WITHOUT USING DRUGS OR ALCOHOL.

Referring to your list of your top five triggers, use the exercise to develop coping strategies to help you avoid engaging in risky behavior when the trigger arises.

Trigger # 1 _____

How can I cope with this without using/drinking?

ANS. _____
_____
_____
_____
_____

Trigger # 2 _____

How can I cope with this without using/drinking?

ANS. _____
_____
_____
_____

Trigger # 3 _____

How can I cope with this without using/drinking?

ANS. _____
_____
_____
_____

Trigger #4 _____

How can I cope with this without using/drinking?

ANS. _____

_____

_____

_____

Trigger # 5 _____

How can I cope with this without using/drinking?

ANS. _____

_____

_____

_____

Most of you came up with more than five triggers. On a separate piece of paper come up with coping strategies for the other triggers that you have written down.

CHAPTER 10

IS CHANGE POSSIBLE?

COMBATING ADDICTION THROUGH RECOVERY EDUCATION

THE C.A.R.E. PROGRAM

IS CHANGE POSSIBLE?

Very simply put, yes, change is possible. Change is a process just as becoming addicted is a process. Nobody suddenly wakes up one morning and declares that they would like to become an alcoholic or an addict. It happened over a period of time.

No matter what your age when you began using, as you drank or used drugs your tolerance grew and you started to use more in order to get the same effects that you had gotten previously. For some people this process takes years and for many others it may happen in a very short period of time.

Either way, just as becoming addicted is a process, so is getting well. It doesn't just happen. What we want to give you is a foundation to build on. Just as a house requires a solid foundation so does your recovery.

So in this portion of the book we are going to look at what is involved in changing lifestyles and what we can expect to experience while making changes.

FEELINGS ASSOCIATED WITH MAKING CHANGES

When changing a behavior that we have engaged in for years we can expect to feel somewhat uncomfortable. After all, you are working on giving up a crutch that you have relied upon heavily.

There is a range of feelings that often go along with making lifestyle changes, some of them very unpleasant. This next exercise will demonstrate how this works and what some of the feelings are that you can expect.

There is three stages here, (**using** drugs and/or alcohol, **transition** (meaning thinking about making changes, actually beginning to make changes or early sobriety) and actually being **clean and sober.**

USING	TRANSITION	CLEAN/SOBER
paranoid	confused	peace of mind
guilt	anger	contentment
insecure	frustrated	secure
low self-esteem	overly emotional	confident
worthless	scared	happy
sick	lonely	sense of belonging
	going crazy	calm
	anxiety	in control
	depression	joyful

As you can see neither the feelings associated with using or transition are particularly pleasant. However, when we get over to the clean and sober side things drastically change. Some of you may be asking, yes but how do I get there? Well, remember recovery is a process; it takes time, one day at a time.
Remember back to the section on physical and psychological dependence. Your body and mind becomes used to functioning while using drugs and/or alcohol. So, transition is not easy, some people have said that they felt like they were going crazy.

It is important to know that this is not the case; your body and mind are going through changes, learning to live substance free. You are not losing your mind, this will pass and you will move into the recovery phase and over time you will begin to experience the pleasant feelings as listed under clean/sober.

CHAPTER 11
NEGATIVE FEELINGS, VALUES AND SUBSTANCE USE

COMBATING ADDICTION THROUGH RECOVERY EDUCATION

THE C.A.R.E. PROGRAM

VALUES, NEGATIVE FEELINGS AND SUBSTANCE USE

Many people whom use and/or abuse substances do so to escape negative feelings. In many circumstances people bring these negative feelings on by themselves. If you are to become and/or remain substance free, you need to begin addressing and reducing the negative feelings that may trigger substance use.

If your behavior is not in line with what you value, negative feelings will arise. This next exercise is intended to identify what it is you value, what's important to you, and then to see if your behavior is in line with those values.

Once your behavior begins to coincide with your values, negative feelings begin to be replaced by more positive ones, thus making it easier to continue living a healthy lifestyle without the use of drugs or alcohol.

On the left hand side of the next diagram you will see a list of values that many people find important to them. On the right you will see the behavior exhibited due to living an unhealthy lifestyle. The direct contradiction between values and behavior caused by an out of control lifestyle is the main contributor of the negative feelings you see in the middle of the diagram.

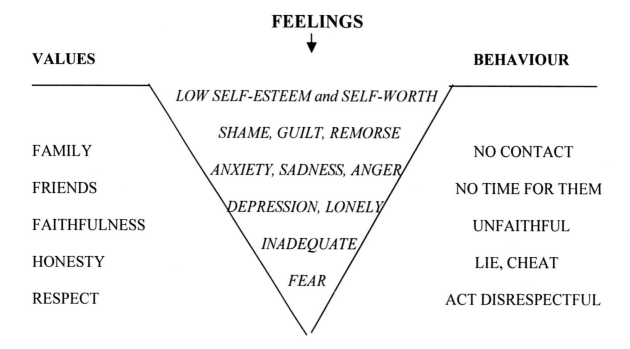

The next diagram shows how drastically our feelings change from negative to positive once we get our behavior in line with what we value.

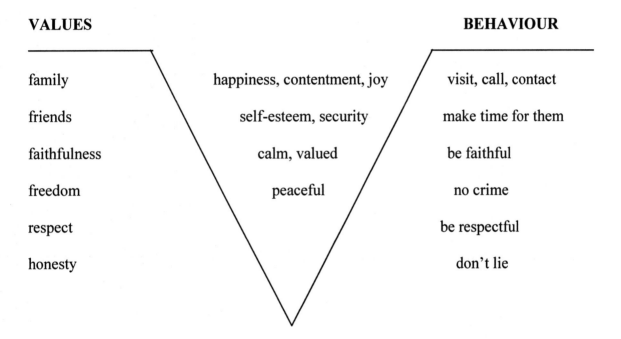

What is a value?
A value is something that is important to you. Something that is part of your belief system.

Examples of values – family, friends, honesty, loyalty, respect, good work ethic, time spent with loved ones, health, fitness, and sobriety.

Now make a list of ten values that are important to you.

_____
_____
_____
_____
_____
_____
_____
_____
_____
_____

From the above list pick the five values that are the most important to you and write them on the following page. Now look at your behavior. Is it in line with what you value?

MY VALUES	**MY BEHAVIOR**
1. _____	_____
2. _____	_____
3. _____	_____
4. _____	_____
5. _____	_____

Negative feelings are one of the major triggers for substance abuse. Once you get your behavior to coincide with your values, negative feelings begin to be replaced by positive ones, thus reducing your risk of relapse.

Transfer your five above values to the next exercise and then write down what you can do to bring your behavior in line with your values. It is not enough to simply write about it. Remember, recovery takes work. Put your new behavior into action starting NOW.

VALUE #1 _____

Actions you can take to bring you closer to living up to your value.

_____

_____

_____

VALUE #2 _____

Actions you can take to bring you closer to living up to your value.

_____

_____

_____

VALUE #3 _____

Actions you can take to bring you closer to living up to your value.

_____

_____

_____

VALUE #4 _____

Actions you can take to bring you closer to living up to your value.

_____

_____

_____

VALUE #5 _____

Actions you can take to bring you closer to living up to your value.

_____

_____

_____

You have made a beginning now by writing out what you can do to bring your behavior more in line with what it is that you value. So, what are you waiting for? Been putting off writing that letter? Have you been making excuses not to call a loved one? Have you been afraid to call a creditor out of fear of what may happen?

I know people, myself included, that had to call a creditor and explain what they were trying to do. That they were trying to straighten their lives out. Honesty is key here. It was amazing the way the creditors stepped up to the plate and offered to help set up a repayment plan. As long as they don't think you are trying to duck them or hide from your responsibility, many of your creditors will try to work with you. In my case I still wound up declaring bankruptcy because I was just into my creditors way over my head.

For many of you it may be too early or your head still not clear enough to really put all your effort into this. Don't worry, do what you can as you can. Then when you begin to feel stronger get at this task in a serious manner. You will not regret it. I guarantee it. If some of the tasks seem very intimidating to you have a support person with you during the tough parts.

CHAPTER 12
SEEKING SUPPORT

COMBATING ADDICTION THROUGH RECOVERY EDUCATION

THE C.A.R.E. PROGRAM

SEEKING SUPPORT

Now is a good time to talk about support systems. Staying clean and sober is not an easy task. Often it is wise to seek out the support of others. I know in my early sobriety it would have been very difficult to remain sober without the love and support of other people in recovery.

I remember lying in a hospital bed after I almost died from an overdose of alcohol and prescription drugs. At the time my best friend's mother (we'll call her Eva) was involved with Alcoholics Anonymous. One day while lying in that hospital bed I turned my head and saw Eva walk through the door. All she said was "come on, I have some friends I want you to meet". She got me out of that hospital bed and took me up to the fourth floor. We walked into this room and there was about 50 people milling about, talking and laughing. There were all ages and types of people there, from housewives to businessmen to people who were obviously down on their luck.

People were coming up to me and shaking my hand and saying things like we are glad you are here, and please come back again. I was in awe, these people seemed like they genuinely cared. I took a seat along with everyone else and the chairman began to call on people to speak. These people were telling my story, they had been where I had been and were recovering. Some had twenty years clean and sober and some had two months. The thing they all had in common was that they were there to support each other.

I remember feeling like I finally fit somewhere. These people understood me and wanted to help. The thing is you have to be willing to allow them to help and I wasn't quite there yet. I spent the next five years going in and out of Alcoholics Anonymous. Each time I went back to drinking, things only got worse so I would go back to A.A. The people there would welcome me back, never saying an unkind word about what I had been up to. After five years of doing this I finally went to a treatment center for 28 days of intensive inpatient treatment.

I have not had to take a drink now since February 28th, 1991. I owe a great debt of gratitude to those people in Alcoholics Anonymous. I will never forget them.

At this point I also need to mention that although I had a life saving experiencing with AA, I also realize that groups such as Alcoholics Anonymous and Narcotics Anonymous are not for everyone. What works for one person may not work for the next. If you do go to a meeting of AA or NA I recommend that you go with an open mind, listen to what others have to say, and do not be too quick to place judgment upon those in attendance and the meeting itself.

Allow those in attendance to accept you and love you until you can accept and love yourself. If you are not comfortable at a particular meeting, go to another one. There are literally thousands of meetings to choose from. Perhaps you live in an area where access to a meeting is not an option. This should rarely happen, as AA is in almost every community worldwide. If this is the case you do have other options for support, below I have listed some other options that may be available to you.

1. Community Service Agencies – usually found in your phone book and often offer various forms of outpatient counseling and support for those trying to recover from substance abuse.

2. Your local hospital or medical clinic – if they do not offer programs of their own they should have a list of agencies that you can contact.

3. Detox Centers – offer inpatient short-term assistance with detoxification. Professionally staffed.

4. Inpatient treatment centers – professionally staffed, offer treatment programs that can run anywhere from 28 days to months in length. Great for giving you a strong foundation upon which to base your recovery.

5. Supportive recovery houses – the ones I know of offer support and camaraderie from other recovering alcoholics and addicts.

6. Health professionals – physicians, psychologists, counselors.

7. Self help groups – Alcoholics Anonymous, Narcotics Anonymous, Rational Recovery.

If in your area you have a counselor who deals specifically with alcohol and drug recovery, contact them. They will be a wealth of information as to what is available in your area.

I would be amiss here if I did not speak to the concept of harm reduction. For those people who are heroin dependent there is methadone maintenance treatment. Methadone keeps the addict from going into withdrawal once heroin consumption is stopped. Methadone reduces the cravings associated with heroin use thus creating an atmosphere where the heroin addict can get help without resorting to the daily grind of an active addict.

This form of treatment needs to be supervised by a health professional and is prescribed by a physician who is licensed to do so. Methadone maintenance therapy should also be accompanied by substance abuse counseling. If you think this may be an option for you, talk to a physician or counselor about this possibility.

Now I have an assignment for you. Find out what is available in your area that could help you. Recovery from drugs and alcohol is a tough road to walk alone. There is help out there. Why not take advantage of it?

AGENCIES AND SERVICES THAT I CAN UTILIZE.
(Include name of agency, ph. number, and address)

_____
_____
_____
_____
_____
_____
_____
_____
_____

CHAPTER 13

GOAL SETTING

COMBATING ADDICTION THROUGH RECOVERY EDUCATION

THE C.A.R.E. PROGRAM

GOAL SETTING

We as human beings need goals in our life. They keep life exciting and new. Without goals people become complacent, lazy, and more apt to pass the time by indulging in the very thing that is destroying them, substance abuse.

What is a goal?
A goal is something to strive for, something you want to accomplish, something you have always wanted to do, or something new that you would like to try.

Having goals to work towards;
- keeps us focused
- keeps us on track
- keeps us motivated
- keeps us productive
- gives us a sense of accomplishment when we reach our goal
- increases self-esteem

Goals are a way of identifying where we want to go and how we are going to get there.

Your priority at this point should be your abstinence from drugs and alcohol, for without it any other goals you have for yourself will be very difficult if not impossible to achieve.

When setting goals for yourself it is suggested that you refer to the acronym SMART.

GOALS NEED TO BE:

S - SPECIFIC, **Detail your goal, do not be vague, exactly what do you want to accomplish. Not just I want to go back to school, be more specific. What do you want to take, what grade, where?**

M – MEASURABLE, **you need to have a way of measuring to know if you are making progress.**

A – ACHEIVABLE, **must be something you can do, something you can accomplish.**

R – REALISTIC, **your goals must be realistic, anything else will only cause frustration.**

T – TIMELY, **is it the right time to be setting this goal and working towards it? Do not frustrate yourself by trying to accomplish something that is not possible at this time.**

If we set nonspecific, unattainable, and unrealistic goals for ourselves we can become anxious, angry, and frustrated, all of which can be triggers for substance use. So when setting goals for yourself make sure they are *realistic, attainable, and specific.*

SHORT AND LONG TERM GOALS

There are 2 types of goals we can set for ourselves, ***short term and long term.***

- Short-term goals are those we would like to accomplish in the very near future.
    - Example - Applying to go to school to take a specific course.
- Long-term goals are those that we would like to accomplish further down the road (1 to 5 years and beyond)
    - Example – completing your degree

The accomplishment of goals we set for ourselves requires taking specific steps. The first thing we need to do is define what the goal is. Once we have done that we need to identify the steps we need to take along the way. It is also helpful to set a timeframe for accomplishment. These are the small steps that we take along the way to achieving our goals.

The outline for goal setting is;

1. **– Write out specifically what the goal is that you want to accomplish.**

2. **- Write down the date you would like to accomplish this by.**

3. **- Write out the steps that you need to take in order of priority.**
   Leave room to write down names of contacts, phone numbers, dates etc.

Example

Goal – To see my family doctor and make him/her aware of my chemical dependency and ask for his/her support during my recovery.

<u>STEPS</u>	<u>DATES & PH. NO's.</u>	
1. Make doctors appointment.	Make appointment by Tues. the 5th Dr. Brown Ph. 555-5555	☐

2. Write down my concerns
   - how long using
   - drug of choice
   (honesty is the key)
	By next Sunday the 3rd	☐

3. Call supportive friend and ask them to come with me for support	by next Monday the 4th Nancy Ph. 000-0000	☐

Check off each step as you complete it   X

Can you see how this is very simply laid out yet gives you specific steps to follow and a time frame to complete them by. Keep track of your progress. Be proud of yourself as you accomplish each step along the way. In order to see how well this works I would like you to do the following goal setting exercise.

GOAL SETTING

Write out as many goals for yourself as you can think of. Then number the goals in order of importance to you. Remember, these are your goals, if they are meaningful to you, you will be more inclined to pursue them.

My goals are	Priority
1. _____	_____
2. _____	_____
3. _____	_____
4. _____	_____
5. _____	_____
6. _____	_____
7. _____	_____
8. _____	_____
9. _____	_____
10. _____	_____

Now pick out your top 3 goals from the previous exercise and write them out fully in the following format. Then identify the steps you need to take while working towards accomplishing the goals you have identified. Where applicable write down the dates you would like to complete certain steps by.

GOAL SETTING

Achieving goals requires the completion of small steps along the way.
Take your time, think about the small steps that need to be taken while working towards your goal.

My #1 goal is _____

STEPS	*CONTACTS & Ph. NO's*
_____	_____
_____	_____
_____	_____
_____	_____
_____	_____
_____	_____
_____	_____

My #2 goal is _____

STEPS	*CONTACTS & Ph. NO's*
_____	_____
_____	_____
_____	_____
_____	_____
_____	_____
_____	_____
_____	_____
_____	_____
_____	_____

My #3 goal is _____

_____

_____

STEPS	**CONTACTS & Ph. NO's**

By now you should be beginning to know what you want and a little about how you are going to get there. Setting goals is great but it is not enough to just write them down. Now you have to put all that writing into action. Unless you stay clean and sober, the chances of any of your goals becoming reality is very slim. So remember, sobriety first and the rest will follow providing you are willing to put in the effort. This may seem like a lot of work but I guess it depends on how badly you want something. When I began writing this book it was a facilitator's manual. Then one small step at a time my dream of writing a book that may help others became a reality. Your goals can become a reality as well. Have faith in yourself and go after them. From what I know this is our one kick at the can. Maybe we get to go around again but I'm not sure. This being the case, don't hold back. Get clean and sober, stay clean and sober, and go after your dreams.

CHAPTER 14
ANGER MANAGEMENT

COMBATING ADDICTION THROUGH RECOVERY EDUCATION

THE C.A.R.E. PROGRAM

ANGER MANAGEMENT

When the whole focus of this book surrounds recovery from chemical dependency why would I include a section on anger management? The answer is very easy. Uncontrolled anger can be a trigger for substance use/abuse.

Have you or anyone you know ever gone out and gotten drunk or high because you were angry?

Have you or anyone you know ever gotten high or drunk at someone then blamed it on him or her? Have you ever purposely started an argument so that you could storm out and go get drunk or high? Think about it. I bet that even if you weren't aware of what you were doing you have engaged in this type of behavior at one time or another.

Examples

- If you had that lousy boss, you'd drink too.
- If you were married to him/her you would get high as well.
- If you had to go to that stinking job everyday you'd go straight to the bar afterward.

Anger is a very complex emotion that has many different meanings and causes. If left uncontrolled, anger has the power to destroy lives. Marriage breakdown, job loss, incarceration, and even suicide are often the result of uncontrolled anger.

That doesn't mean that anger does not have a useful purpose. Anger is known as an arousal response. It alerts us through physiological and psychological changes that something is not right.

Anger cues – changes we notice in our bodies and minds that are a signal that something is not right, that we are beginning to escalate.

Examples of anger cues are:

- muscles tense
- heart rate increases
- volume of voice changes
- rapid breathing
- thoughts race
- feeling flushed
- pacing
- clenching fist and jaw muscles

Now take a few minutes and write down your own anger cues. Write down as many as you can think of.

PERSONAL ANGER CUES

Think of the anger cues you experience when you are getting angry. Do your muscles tense? Does your stomach get upset? Write down as many of your personal anger cues as you can think of.

MY PERSONAL ANGER CUES

1. _____
2. _____
3. _____
4. _____
5. _____
6. _____

7. _____

8. _____

9. _____

10. _____

There is a cycle to our anger and the resulting consequences from it. We do not just all of a sudden go off the deep end and become extremely angry.
Even if we don't recognize it, there is always a trigger that sets the anger cycle in motion.

Everyone's triggers for anger can be different but a few examples are:
- someone cutting you off in traffic
- a spouse being untruthful
- people not cleaning up after themselves
- being mistreated

What triggers your anger?

_____
_____
_____
_____
_____

SAY – After the trigger phase there is 4 other phases to the anger cycle that we go through. The following will explain these phases.

We experience anger in our bodies as well as our minds. As we begin to experience angry thoughts and feelings, our bodies begin to prepare for action. The following graph illustrates our body's response.

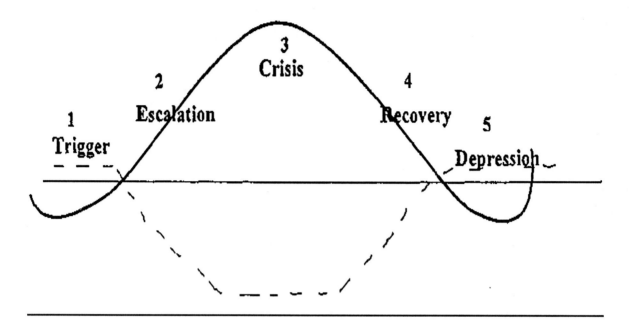

The Trigger Phase

An event usually triggers the rest of the anger cycle. This could be an argument, a physical attack, or some information that shocks you. You feel threatened and you begin getting ready to meet the challenge.

For example, you are out for a walk and suddenly and an object that was thrown from the bushes strikes you from behind. In this example, the trigger was external but triggers can also be created internally through memory, perception or your stress level.

The Escalation Phase

During the Escalation Phase we actually make ourselves angrier through our self-talk. Example – I can't believe it, that so and so, I'm going to get them for this. Now the body's arousal systems begins preparing for a crisis. The body prepares to attack or defend itself by pumping adrenaline into the blood stream.

The Crisis Phase

This phase begins with the "fight or flight" crisis. The body has maximized its preparation and a physiological command is issued, "take action!" Either get out of here or prepare to do battle!! Unfortunately, our quality of judgment is reduced and decisions are not made with clarity of mind.

The Recovery Phase

The crisis is over. We have done what we can to resolve the situation. Breathing returns to normal and we begin to calm down. Clarity of thought begins to return.

The Post Crisis Depression Phase

After reviewing the situation and assessing what just occurred if we find we have acted inappropriately feelings of guilt, regret, and depression arrive on the scene. As alcoholics and addicts this is especially dangerous.

It is during and after the post crisis depression phase that you are often at risk for a slip or relapse. There are many negative feelings that go along with the post crisis depression phase. Feelings such as guilt, sadness, and depression.

How does an alcoholic or addict deal with negative feelings? They pick up and use. That is the one way we have always handled negative feelings in the past. We do this because it has temporarily worked and brought us relief. It temporarily negates the negative feelings. Now we need to find a way to not only handle our feelings and emotions differently, we need to look at ways of avoiding putting ourselves in situations that create the feelings we are looking to numb.

One way to do this is to get out of the anger cycle early, at the trigger phase. This way we avoid going through the rest of the cycle and help lower the risk of resorting to substance use/abuse. As soon as we begin to feel triggered or recognize cues that we are getting angry we must do something about it, we must get out of the cycle.

Below are some methods of interrupting the anger cycle that have proven to be effective for people who utilize them.

THE TIME OUT

The "time-out" is a simple yet effective tool for dealing with angry feelings and behavior. The intention of the "time-out" is not to offer long-term solutions to conflict and anger problems. This tool is simply intended to offer a short- term alternative to behavior that can be destructive to you and others, and to defuse situations that could lead to a slip or relapse.

The "time-out" is a technique that requires practice and commitment. Initial obstacles to taking a "time-out" may not be foreseen and so it is sometimes recommended that a practice "time-out" should take place before a real one is necessary.

THERE ARE FOUR STEPS TO THE "TIME-OUT"

1. Practice getting in touch with your anger cues so that you are aware of when you are getting angry. Identify that you are escalating to the point where you need to get out of the situation.

2. Decide to take the "time-out" before your anger escalates to the point where it is difficult to leave the situation. Indicate to the other person/persons that you are leaving. Do not make any long speeches at this point. Simply indicate that you are taking a time out. (If your anger at times happens in personal relationships make sure you inform the other parties about the time out in advance).

3. Leave where you are and get away from the situation. If you are not already outside, go outside where there is fresh air. Do not simply go to another room of the house or workplace. It is important that you physically leave the site of the conflict. Don't get "hooked" into staying in the conflict. Take 1/2 to 1 hour to calm down and get your thoughts together. If you need longer let the other person/persons know this. Do not "stomp-out" or make cutting remarks on your way out.

4. Return and decide with the person/persons that you had the conflict with whether or not to return to the discussion or issue that took place before you left.

DURING THE TIME OUT

DO NOT	**DO**
Drink/do drugs	Think of other things
Talk to unhealthy people	Walk/cycle/run
Rehearse the argument	Talk to positive support
Drive	Come back in 1 hour

USING POSITIVE SELF TALK TO REDUCE ANGER

Before entering a situation that you know might provoke you:

"This may be difficult, but I know how to deal with it."
    "I can plan to handle this, take it easy and think."
    "Remember, stick to the issues and don't take it personally."
    "There is no need for an argument, I can to handle this constructively."

During a provocation:

"The only person I can control is myself, I don't need to control the other person."
"I won't make more out of this than I have to."
"There is no point in getting mad. I can plan how to deal with this in an appropriate manner."
"I need to be careful not to make assumptions. I will get the facts first."

Reducing my anger:

"I recognize my anger cues. STOP!! Think about what to do next."
"I'm getting tense, relax and slow down."
"My anger is telling me something is wrong. Time to do some problem solving."
"I am going to take a time out, then I will come back and deal with this."

TALK TO SOMEONE

Find a supportive person to talk to. Get a hold of a friend, family member, clergy, elder or counselor. If you can't find someone to talk to write about your feelings. Don't just let them boil up inside you. Anger left to simmer becomes a volcano.

CHAPTER 15

CONFLICT RESOLUTION

COMBATING ADDICTION THROUGH RECOVERY EDUCATION

THE C.A.R.E. PROGRAM

CONFLICT RESOLUTION

THE BASIC RULES

You've got a disagreement on your hands and it's turning into a full-scale conflict. Emotions are starting to run high – anger, distrust, resentment, defensiveness, fear, and rejection are evident.

You're first job is to defuse the situation. Here are some basic rules for creating a respectful and productive atmosphere.

DON'T INTERUPT

- Let each person have his or her say.

DON'T PASS JUDGEMENTS

- Avoid name calling or labeling, they just make the situation worse.

STAY FOCUSED ON THE PRESENT SITUATION

- Don't bring up past difficulties or situations.

DEAL WITH ONLY ONE ISSUE AT A TIME

- If the problem is bigger than just one issue and other issues crop up, agree to break it into smaller portions. This makes the main issue more manageable.

GIVE YOURSELF ENOUGH TIME –

- Don't rush the process. Take your time, think about what is actually going on.

AFTER DEALING WITH THE SITUATION:

a. **Conflict unresolved:**

"Forget about the aggravation. If it can't be resolved, let it go."
"After a time-out I will think of a constructive way to deal with it."
"Shake it off, life is too short."
"Who can I call? I need to talk to someone positive."

b. **Conflict resolved:**

"I handled that pretty well, I could have gotten upset but I didn't."
"I am getting much better at controlling myself"
"I'm going to remember how I coped with that situation, it may be useful again"

CHAPTER 16
COMMUNICATION

COMBATING ADDICTION THROUGH RECOVERY EDUCATION

THE C.A.R.E. PROGRAM

COMMUNICATION

Being an effective communicator is a skill that is mastered with practice. Being able to communicate effectively is essential in today's world. It is far more than being able to talk. It is being able to listen. It is how you conduct yourself. It is about respect.

Why do you think we would include a section on communication in a substance abuse program?

Answer – Because miscommunication is a direct cause of frustration, anger, and anxiety. All of which can be a precursor to substance use.

It is important to be an effective communicator because:

- there are less miss-understandings
- saves frustration
- avoids confusion
- creates self-esteem
- people respect you and you develop self-respect

LISTENING SKILLS

A difficult part of effective communication is listening to hear what the other person is saying. Have you ever been in a conversation but in your mind been somewhere else? Before you know it you have missed what the conversation is all about. We are all guilty of this from time to time. If someone has something to say to us it is obviously important to the other person. Try not to drift off and be fishing, or at the mall, or reliving a past experience during conversations. Give that person your attention.

TIPS FOR EFFECTIVE LISTENING

1. **Give the other person your complete attention; do not be drifting off elsewhere.**

2. Do not interrupt, be respectful, and wait until the other person is done and then offer your part of the conversation.

3. If someone has something important to discuss stop what you are doing. Close your book. Turn off the TV. If you are at work or elsewhere and there are many distractions around try to find a quiet spot for your conversation.

4. Use paraphrasing if you are not clear on what the other person is saying. (paraphrasing) – repeating back to the person in your own words what you believe they said -- "So if I hear you right you are saying _____." The other person will either say yes, or they will say no and clarify the point they are trying to get across.

Here are a few more tips that are particularly helpful when engaging in important matters such as a job interview, an important meeting, or any other situation where you want to be seen as polite, interested, and respectful.

- SIT SQUARELY, face the person directly that you are in conversation with.

- BE **O**PEN, do not sit with your arms tightly crossed. Be open, it makes you look interested.

- LEAN FORWARD, lean forward a little, it makes you appear involved and interested.

- MAKE EYE CONTACT, try to maintain eye contact with the person you are talking to.

- RELAX, don't be fidgeting around, if you are nervous before entering the meeting or discussion, take a deep breath, talk to someone or go for a short walk.

CHAPTER 17

DEALING WITH RESENTMENT

COMBATING ADDICTION THROUGH RECOVERY EDUCATION

THE C.A.R.E. PROGRAM

DEALING WITH RESENTMENT

Holding onto resentments is one of the main reasons that alcoholics and addicts continue to use and/or relapse. We must rid ourselves of these resentments that we hold or they can kill others or us. Many assaults stem from a grudge or resentment.

Resentment is ill feelings we hold towards another person, place, or situation. We often hold onto these ill feelings and allow them to grow and fester within us.

Having and holding onto resentment is like having an infection. The longer you have an infection without treating it the worse it gets. The infection gradually takes over and infects your entire being. In order to remain healthy we must do what is necessary to get the infection out of our system.

HOW DO WE FREE OURSELVES OF RESENTMENT?

Ask yourself this question. When I hold resentment towards a person, place, or institution, who is really getting hurt? Usually the person, place, thing, or situation that we have resentment towards is not even aware that we hold the resentment. While we are tossing and turning and cannot sleep the other person is totally unaware that we are bothered. We are the only ones who get hurt when we hold resentment towards another.

In order to help you let go of resentment try the following suggestions.

- Use thinking skills to cope.
  What is the bottom line here, who am I really mad at?
  Can you change the situation or is it out of your control?
  If it is out of your control stop beating yourself up, let it go.
  Are you making more out of the situation than is necessary?

- Talk to someone who is healthy that you trust. Tell them what is bothering you. Ask for some honest feedback. Talking about things takes the power away from them.

- Get some paper and write it out, get all your feelings out on paper. Try not to miss any important details.

- If you are a spiritual person ask the God of your understanding to remove the resentment. Do this everyday until you are free of it.

- If necessary get counseling. Do not allow the resentment to slowly eat away at you.

Resentment left to fester and grow has caused many alcoholics and addicts to relapse.

CHAPTER 18

RELAPSE PREVENTION PLAN

COMBATING ADDICTION THROUGH RECOVERY EDUCATION

THE C.A.R.E. PROGRAM

MY RELAPSE PREVENTION PLAN

This is my personal relapse prevention plan. I make a commitment to myself to refer to this plan often and utilize the tools I have learned. In this way I will be able to remain abstinent and enjoy all that life has to offer. To begin with I will list my top five triggers and ways that I can cope with them in a healthy manner.

Triggers are people, places, and things that can increase my risk of returning to substance use. Sharing this plan with someone will help make it more meaningful. I choose to share my plan with _____.

Trigger #1 _____

How can I cope with this (thoughts / actions taken).
_____
_____
_____
_____
_____
_____

Trigger #2 _____

How can I cope with this (thoughts / actions taken).

_____
_____
_____
_____
_____
_____
_____

Trigger #3 _____

How can I cope with this (thoughts / actions taken).

_____
_____
_____
_____
_____
_____
_____

Trigger #4 _____

How can I cope with this (thoughts / actions taken).

_____
_____
_____
_____
_____
_____
_____

Trigger #5 _____

How can I cope with this (thoughts / actions taken)?
_____
_____
_____
_____
_____
_____

Staying clean from drugs and alcohol requires work. Remember that many of us used to go to any lengths to use. Now we must go to any lengths to stay clean and sober.
Am I prepared to do whatever it takes to stay clean and sober? ANSWER _____

MY ONGOING RECOVERY PLAN

What I will do on a daily basis for my recovery?
MONDAY: _____
_____

TUESDAY: _____
_____

WEDNESDAY: _____
_____

THURSDAY: _____
_____

FRIDAY: _____
_____

SATURDAY: _____
_____

SUNDAY: _____
_____

What I will do on a weekly basis for my recovery?

_____
_____
_____
_____
_____
_____
_____
_____
_____
_____
_____
_____

Being clean and sober requires having balance in life. Below are other areas of my life and my description of what I will do to ensure that I am a well-rounded person.

What I will do for fun

_____
_____
_____
_____
_____
_____
_____

Socializing

_____
_____
_____

___

___

___

___

___

___

___

___

___

Spirituality

___

___

___

___

___

___

___

___

___

___

Family Activities

___

___

___

___

___

___

___

___

___

Work

_____
_____
_____
_____
_____
_____
_____
_____
_____

Relaxation

_____
_____
_____
_____
_____
_____
_____
_____
_____

Staying clean and sober is easier if we have the support of others to help us through the difficult times. We also need people we can rely upon if we need to contact them in times of turmoil. Below is a list of people and places that I can turn to should I need help with staying abstinent.

_____
_____
_____
_____

My Relapse Prevention Plan ~ 127

_____
_____
_____
_____
_____
_____
_____
_____
_____
_____
_____
_____

I know that A.A. and N.A. are not for everyone. However, I plan on attending ____ A.A., N.A., or other recovery based meetings per week.

If not attending A.A. or N.A. I make a commitment to meet with a supportive person at least once per week.

Name, address, date and time of the meeting/s I plan on attending.

_____
_____
_____
_____
_____
_____
_____
_____
_____

I know that A.A. and N.A. both recommend that I get a sponsor.

Do I have a sponsor? _____

Am I going to get a sponsor? _____

SPONSOR'S NAME AND PHONE NUMBER.

_____
_____
_____

CHAPTER 19

JOURNALING

COMBATING ADDICTION THROUGH RECOVERY EDUCATION

THE C.A.R.E. PROGRAM

JOURNALING

You may or may not have kept a journal before. If you haven't, a journal is where you can put your thoughts on paper. This helps make sense of the confusing neighborhood we call our mind, and I know your neighborhood is a little confused right now. Writing about things helps take the power away from them. Don't know where to start? Some say it is good to write at the end of the day. I found that whenever I felt the need was the right time. Just start by writing about your day, or what you are feeling. Get your frustration out on paper.

I always took my journal to my therapist and read it to her. This was very helpful because this is where my true feelings were, on the paper. You have room to start here. You will probably find after awhile that you feel so much better after journaling that you will want to keep going. Get yourself a separate book just for this purpose.

_____
_____
_____
_____
_____
_____
_____

CONCLUSION

Well, you have taken a big step. Be proud of yourself. You are beginning to take a look at a problem that no one likes to face. Truthfully though, the work has just begun. The hard work is going to be living life on life's terms without your crutch. Remember though, your chemical dependency may have started out as your best friend but it turned into your worst enemy.

If while reading and working through this book you took an honest look at yourself and you didn't like what you saw, don't despair. All that mess and confusion was the addiction rearing its ugly head. Now it is up to you to turn things around. You have the power to do so. Don't ever give up. It is when we give up and give in that we lose. Keep fighting for your life. It is worth it. If you still have your family, your job, and some money in the bank, you are very fortunate. Keep drinking and/or using drugs and you will likely lose everything that means anything to you, probably sooner than you think.

You thought enough about yourself to pick up this book. Now reach out and access some of the other help that is available. If possible get to a support group or a therapist. Open up to someone, talk, talk, talk. Get rid of the poison you have been keeping inside. If you put half the energy into your recovery as you put into your using, you will be well on your way to a full and satisfying life.

Believe me when I say you are in my heart and prayers as you continue forth on your journey. I know you can do this. Peace be with you.

Printed in the United States
23577LVS00003B/67-90